T0156770

Medicine Bow...
A New Beginning

Sally Campbell Repass

authorHOUSE®

AuthorHouse™
1663 Liberty Drive
Bloomington, IN 47403
www.authorhouse.com
Phone: 1-800-839-8640

Published by AuthorHouse 10/26/12

ISBN: 978-1-4772-8418-6 (sc)
ISBN: 978-1-4772-8416-2 (e)

Contents

Chapter 1

Rachel Hargrove met and married Dr. Mitch Parker. They had a wonderful life together for five years. He was killed in a car accident one night on the way home from work. This was to have been a special night for them as she had a surprise waiting for him. She was going to tell him that she was finally going to have a baby after years of trying. He never made it home so she lived with the guilt of not telling him as soon as she found out. Her baby girl, Jennifer Rose Parker, was born seven months later.

When Jennifer was a few years old Rachel met and married Grayson Sterling. They had a wonderful life together and had a son, Robert Grayson Sterling, Jr. and a daughter Miranda Noelle Sterling.

During those years they found out that Jennifer had twin half brothers, Jordan Hoffsteader and Blake Parker. They were raised a world apart. These were the sons of Mitch Parker. He had three children and never knew about any of them.

Jennifer became a doctor following in her dad's footsteps. Her mom, Rachel, died from ovarian cancer before Jennifer finished medical school.

Miranda became a Veterinarian and moved to Prince Edward Island to become partners with Dr. Laura Fisher at PETS PARADISE CLINIC. She met and married Mardi Carson while living there.

Rob became a lawyer and married Kati Campbell from Prince Edward Island. They remained living there on the island and had a son Robert Grayson Sterling III.

Jennifer married an actor while living in California going to medical school, and this marriage ended in divorce. She later married her high school sweetheart Gabe Colter. She was on top of the world. They had twins, Isac and Isabelle. When the children were six years old, Isac, was killed when he was thrown from his pony. This was a terrible tragedy to the family. Grayson blamed himself for the accident and never got over the death of his grandson.

Miranda and Mardi moved back to Montana to live on the ranch to help take care of her aging dad, Grayson Sterling. Six months later he died in his sleep. Miranda was the one to find him and had a terrible time dealing with this.

Then an unknown cousin, Caycee Canfield, a fashion designer from New York, entered into their life like a whirlwind. Taking advantage of the fact that she looked almost exactly like Miranda, she made a play for Miranda's husband Mardi. This did not set well with Miranda. She was ready to kick her out of the house but instead asked her to go to church with them. Caycee accepted the invitation. That was the day she became a Christian. Miranda felt that she did what God would have wanted her to do in befriending Caycee.

Jennifer's friend, Harley Brock, came for a visit and immediately fell in love with Caycee. They had a big beautiful wedding on the ranch. Caycee had asked Mardi to take them for a ride in the carriage, which he did, and that ended in a terrible accident in which Mardi lost his life. Caycee felt responsible for Mardi's death. Had she not entered into their lives, Mardi would most likely still be alive. Miranda knew this and had a hard time dealing with it. She knew she had to let go of the past and not dwell on it. She had to forgive Caycee for what she had done. She knew she had to build another life for herself and her little daughter Taylor Lynn Carson.

Jennifer and Gabe had been blessed with another daughter Rachel Rose Colter, named after Jennifer's mother Rachel. She had filled a void in their life. God had been so good to them. He had taken little Isac but had given them baby Rachel Rose, not as a replacement but as His special gift to them.

Chapter 2

It had been exactly one year since the death of Dr. Miranda Sterling's husband Mardi Carson. It had not been an easy year for Miranda. She went for six months of counseling with Dr. Garth Sable. He had helped her a lot and she was learning to deal with the loss of Mardi and learning to forgive Caycee for all the trouble she had caused. She still felt a void in her life and knew she always would. Having little Taylor who was almost two years old had helped her tremendously. It would have been much harder if she had been completely alone. Jennifer and Gabe had been so good to her and helped her in every way possible. She was so thankful for them!

She had been thinking lately that it might be time for her and Taylor to move away from the Parker Ranch and start a new life of their own. She had too many sad memories on this ranch. She knew it wouldn't be easy but she felt she was intruding in the life of Jennifer and Gabe. They had their family, two beautiful daughters, Isabelle and Rachel Rose. Gabe could continue to run the ranch since he had plenty of good help. She somehow felt like a third wheel. She dreaded bringing up the subject with

Jennifer because she knew what Jennifer would say. She was very close to her sister and would miss her, but she felt it was time to move on.

Later that evening after they all sat down to dinner and said the blessing, Miranda spoke aloud. "Jennifer and Gabe, I have something to say to you both. Words cannot express my feelings of gratitude for all you have done for me this past year. You've been here for me when I could not have made it alone. I thank God every day for both of you and what you mean to me. However, I have been thinking about this for quite some time. I feel like it is time for Taylor and me to leave the ranch and start a new life."

"WHAT?" Jennifer jumped up from the table. "WHERE?"

"I don't know that yet. I haven't decided," replied Miranda.

"Don't be in a hurry. Make sure this is what you really want before you make a decision," said Jennifer. "You know you don't have to go."

"Oh I know that but it's what I feel like I have to do. I just don't know where we're going yet."

"What about your clinic? Are you willing to give that up?" asked Jennifer.

"I can't let that influence me. I have too many memories here and I need to get away from it all. I'm sure I can rent the clinic to another vet."

"Please don't go back to Prince Edward Island!" exclaimed Jennifer.

"Oh I'm not going that far away," laughed Miranda.

"GOOD! Please take your time in making your decision!"

"My mind is made up, Jennifer. I just haven't decided where yet. If I'm lucky I will find someone who needs a partner like Dr. Laura Fisher did. You know I still miss her. She was not only a partner but also a very good friend."

"I know. Laura is a very special lady," added Jennifer.

"Indeed she is! If I can't find a partner I will open up my own clinic. Working with animals is my life and I wouldn't be content doing anything else."

"I know that Miranda! I think you should continue to do what you love and are best suited for. Animals are drawn to you like a magnet. You know I don't want you to go, but if you feel like you have to then I wish you the best. Just keep me updated, okay?"

"You know I will Jennifer!" Miranda exclaimed with a smile. "I would like to take Taylor to a smaller town where people live at a slower pace. I am just tired of all the hustle and bustle of living so close to the city. We can live on much less than we do now. I have been trying to save as much as possible so I do have enough to live on for quite awhile."

"Well that is good!" exclaimed Jennifer. "Let me know when you find that quaint little town."

"You'll be the first to know. I promise."

"Good," replied Jennifer. "Do you have any particular place in mind?"

"Not really," replied Miranda. "I just know I don't want to go too far away, perhaps a few hundred miles. Maybe four or five hours traveling distance."

"I guess that won't be too bad!" exclaimed Jennifer. "At least we can see you more often than when you moved to Prince Edward Island."

"True," added Miranda. "I don't ever want to live that far away from the ranch anymore."

"I'm glad to hear you say that," replied Jennifer with a sigh of relief.

"I plan to do some research on the internet and

hopefully find the perfect place to call home. Meanwhile things will continue as normal here."

"Have you told Sallie yet?"

"No I thought I would wait until I find out where we're going."

"You know she's going to be upset."

"I know that but I have to make a change. I want to relocate before Taylor gets old enough to start school. It will be easier on her."

"I'm already missing you and you aren't even gone yet!" exclaimed a sad looking Jennifer. "Isabelle and Rachel Rose will be lost without Taylor!"

"Are you trying to lay a guilt trip on me my dear sister?" asked a smiling Miranda.

"Not really, I guess I'm just feeling sorry for myself. Oh, and for my children too!"

"You can just get over that," laughed Miranda. "I don't plan to go too far away. You can always come for a visit."

"Indeed I will!" exclaimed Jennifer.

After dinner was over and the dishes were washed, Miranda took Taylor upstairs for her bath, bedtime story, then off to bed. She tucked her precious baby into her crib and sang her a lullaby. Taylor drifted off to sleep and Miranda tiptoed out of the room.

Chapter 3

Miranda retired to her room and turned on the computer. She hardly knew where to begin. She pulled up a map of several different states surrounding Montana and searched the names of many towns. Nothing jumped out at her. She wasn't sure what she was expecting to happen but nothing felt right so far. Two hours later she pulled up a map of Wyoming. She searched it carefully reading the names of all the towns. Just as she was about to call it quits it jumped out at her... MEDICINE BOW.

MEDICINE BOW, WYOMING? She knew nothing about that place. All she knew was that a TV series called 'THE VIRGINIAN' was supposed to have taken place there. Of course she knew it was filmed in Hollywood. After all the searching she had done... this place comes up. She just didn't understand. True, she wanted to go to a smaller place but just how small was this place? She intended to find out. In fact, she planned to find out everything she could about Medicine Bow. For some reason she was intrigued by this place!

She decided to start with the internet. She typed Medicine Bow, Wyoming in the search engine and found several websites. She was excited when she found the General History of Medicine Bow. She read it slowly and took in every word.

The name 'Medicine Bow' is legendary and reputedly derives its origin from the Native American tribes that frequented the area, mainly the Arapaho and Cheyenne. Along the banks of the river the Native Americans found excellent material for making their bows. To them, anything they found good for a purpose was called 'good medicine'. Thus, the Native Americans named the river flowing through the area the Medicine Bow River and since the headwaters of the river originated in the mountains to the South, they were called the 'Medicine Bow Mountains'.

According to the report, the area was first used by trappers and mountain men during the 1830's. In 1868 The Union Pacific Railroad was built through the area and a pumping station was established on the river. A store and saloon were the beginning of the small village which naturally was given the name of 'Medicine Bow'. By the following year Medicine Bow had become a major supply point and in the 1870's, the federal government operated a military post in Medicine Bow to protect the railroad and freight wagons from attack. A post office was built and in 1876, the first elementary school was established.

By the late 1870's and early 1880's, Medicine Bow Livestock Association reported that they had become the largest shipping point for range livestock on the Union Pacific line. Cattle were being brought for shipping from as far away as Idaho and Montana. An average of 2,000 head a day was being shipped. By the turn of the century Medicine Bow was also a major shipping point for wool averaging 1,000 tons a year.

In 1901 the Union Pacific Railroad was relocated from

the Rock Creek route to its present location and a depot was built in Medicine Bow. The original depot burned down July 24, 1913 and the present depot was erected in November 1913.

In 1909 Medicine Bow was incorporated when the Union Pacific Railroad transferred ownership to the town. This was a celebration day for the people.

In late 1913 the transcontinental 'Lincoln Highway' passed right through Medicine Bow. In the 1930's it was paved bringing tourism to the area.

In later years Lumber, Uranium, Coal, and Natural Gas were found in the area which added to the prosperity of the region.

"Wow, this is interesting," thought Miranda. She was going to find out more before making a decision. So she continued her search. She found that the housing costs in Medicine Bow were invitingly low. It seemed they had property for sale in town or outside the town limits, as well as rental homes, apartments, and mobile home lots in town. The Elementary School, Convenience Store, and the Post Office and many other services were all within walking distance no matter where you lived in town. Schools were considered safe and the community had a low crime rate. Miranda thought this was sounding better all the time. This could be the perfect place for her and Taylor.

Medicine Bow is a tiny town, not a city. There are no neighborhoods, no urban or suburban areas. The houses are all located in town. Outside of town, there are only ranches. It seems that living in town here is not much different than living on the outskirts of town elsewhere.

Bring your business to Medicine Bow, said the article. That started the wheels in her mind turning. Why not open a Veterinarian Clinic there? That was something she was definitely going to check out. Another thought entered her mind. She needed to make a trip to Medicine Bow and see for herself. She started looking at her calendar trying to decide a good time to go. First she would have to check her work schedule. Then she would need to see if Sallie could move into the house and stay while she was gone. She was sure that would not be a problem since Sallie loved Taylor so much.

She gave Sallie a call the next morning. "Hello Sallie. Hope things are well with you. I have a proposition for you."

"Really? Just how can I help you?"

"It's a long story, Sallie. I am thinking about moving to Medicine Bow, Wyoming."

"MEDICINE BOW, WYOMING! Am I hearing you correctly?"

"Yes," laughed Miranda. "I know this is kind of sudden to everyone but I have been thinking about leaving the ranch for quite awhile."

"Why in the world would you want to do that?"

"With Mardi gone, I feel like a third wheel to Jennifer and Gabe. I feel that I should make a new life for Taylor and myself."

"What am I going to do without you? Without Taylor? I have gotten so attached to her."

"You can always go with us. In fact that is a brilliant idea. What do you say?"

"This is so sudden. When are you leaving?" asked Sallie.

"I plan to make a trip to Medicine Bow and look things over. I want to see if this is really where I want to live. I know it's a very small place but it might be just what we need."

"I don't know if I could leave Ethel and Emily," sighed Sallie.

"I understand. It will have to be your choice."

"Let me think on it and I will let you know soon. I want to talk to my sisters first."

"Can you move in here and stay while I go for a visit? I shouldn't be gone more than a week."

"Of course I will. You know I would do anything for you and Taylor!"

"Great! Then it's settled. I will start planning my trip. I need to contact someone in Medicine Bow and find out some details. I will let you know as soon as I get my plans made."

"Okay Miranda."

"We'll talk later," said Miranda. "Bye, Sallie!"

"Goodbye, Miranda!"

Miranda hung up the phone and headed for the shower. She was due at work in one hour. She could have talked to Sallie at work but wasn't sure she would have time. She wanted to give her a 'heads up', and give her time to ponder the idea. It would be great if Sallie moved with them. She wouldn't have to look for a new nanny. "Dear God," she prayed, "please work everything out for us. I am trusting in you to provide us with a home, and to heal my broken heart. A new start may be just what I need. So God... take care of everything for us. Thank you! In the name of your Son Jesus I pray. Amen."

Somehow her heart felt lighter. She would survive. With God's help she would make it. She was so thankful for little Taylor who was such a Godsend. She finished dressing then went to get Taylor dressed. They went downstairs and had breakfast. Then it was time to go to the clinic.

Sallie arrived about the same time they did. "Good

morning my two special girls," she said with a smile. "I talked to Emily and Ethel last night. Although they will miss me they actually encouraged me to go with you. I was really surprised. I thought they would talk me out of going."

"That's wonderful!" exclaimed Miranda. "So you'll go?"

"I am planning on it."

"Great! I will know more after my visit to Medicine Bow. Tonight I am going to try to contact someone there. I will keep you updated."

"Thanks Miranda."

It was another ordinary day. Miranda stayed busy with surgery and regular routine visits. She was glad when five o'clock finally came. She rushed home and started dinner. While it was cooking she bathed Taylor and got her ready for bed. That way she would be ready to be tucked into bed after dinner.

With dinner over and Taylor tucked in for the night, Miranda sat down at her computer. She found the Official Website for the Town of Medicine Bow. While searching she found the Town Clerk/Treasurer, Karen Heath. She decided to send her an email with a few questions.

The next evening when she checked her email there was one from Karen in Medicine Bow. Miranda was so excited. The Virginian Hotel seemed to be the place to stay, according to Karen. Miranda immediately called them and made reservations. She would be going there for a visit one week from tomorrow. She decided to drive since it was only about five hours away. She was getting excited. This was the happiest she had been since before Mardi died. In her mind she knew she was doing the right thing. Maybe being in a new place without familiar surroundings would bring closure for her. That's what she was desperately praying for.

She had a lot to do in the few days before leaving. Since Sallie was taking care of Taylor, she would have extra time to get everything done. If things go well and she decides to move to Medicine Bow, she would have to find someone to rent her clinic. In her mind she was sure she would be moving and that was without even seeing the place. Something seemed to be calling her there. They needed her...they had no Veterinarian Clinic in town. She would feel so good being able to help these people and keep them from having to drive to another town for service.

Chapter 4

The day finally came. She was up early and was wide awake even though she never slept much the night before. She was too excited! She had her car packed and was ready to go. She said goodbye to her darling baby and Sallie. It was a tearful goodbye, like she was leaving forever. Since the kidnapping of her baby she was reluctant to let Taylor out of her sight for very long. She trusted Sallie completely and knew Taylor was in good hands. That was such a relief.

Five hours later she arrived in Medicine Bow. She had stopped several times along the way. She pulled into town just before noon. Several people were on the street. She looked around from building to building wondering what some of them were. Then she spotted a small diner on the street corner. She decided to stop there for a quick lunch. She parked her car and got out. As she walked into the diner she glanced around. There were only two vacant tables. She seated herself and waited for a waitress. Soon a cute little redhead approached her table. "Hello, my name is Madison. Here's a menu and I'll be back soon to take your order," she said with a smile.

"Thank you," replied Miranda. She opened the menu

and started reading. Soon she decided on a Chicken Fillet sandwich and a glass of Tea. Madison came back, took her order and left with a smile. Ten minutes later lunch arrived. Miranda thanked her and started to eat. She was starving.

While she was at the counter paying for her lunch she asked for directions to the Virginian Hotel. She was told it was on Route #30 which runs North-South through the town. It was easy to find. She parked her car, grabbed her luggage, and went in the front door.

"Welcome to the Virginian Hotel," said a young man with a big friendly smile.

"Thank you," replied Miranda.

"I'm Jonathan, but everyone calls me Jon. How may I help you?"

"I have reservations for several nights. My name is Miranda Sterling."

"Sterling... Oh yes, here it is."

"You will be in room 204," he said as he handed her the key.

"Thank you, Jon."

"Hope you have a pleasant stay at our wonderful hotel."

"Thanks. I'm really looking forward to my visit in Medicine Bow."

"Special place it is... Medicine Bow. I wouldn't live anywhere else."

"That's interesting to hear, as I am thinking of relocating here."

"Really? Where are you from?" Jon asked.

"I'm from Laurel, Montana."

"Montana, huh? I hear that is a beautiful state."

"Oh it is. I never thought I would ever leave again."

"Again?" Jon asked.

"Oh yeah...I moved to Prince Edward Island a few years ago, then returned to Montana. That's a long story."

"Anyway, we are happy to have you visiting with us and hope you decide you like it enough to relocate."

"Maybe I will, Jon." She smiled and headed for the elevator. It had been a long ride and she was a little tired. She planned to rest for an hour or so before she went exploring. She unlocked the door to her room not knowing what to expect. She was stunned at the beauty. It was done in shades of pink with touches of emerald green. How could they know it was her favorite colors? She laid her luggage on the pale green carpet and turned back the comforter on the bed. She took off her shoes and lay down on the bed. Before she realized it she had slept for two hours. "Mercy me I didn't mean to sleep that long," she said out loud. She jumped up and headed for the bathroom. She combed her hair, touched up her makeup, grabbed her purse, and headed for the door.

She drove a few blocks until she came to the Town Hall where Karen was working. She could hardly wait to meet this lady who had been so nice and helpful to her. As soon as she walked in the door she knew she had found a friend. The beautiful young lady at the desk looked up and gave her the most welcoming smile. "Hello, I'm Karen Heath. You must be Miranda."

"Indeed I am," replied Miranda with a big smile. "It's so nice to meet you, Karen!"

"It's nice to meet you too! I hope you had a pleasant trip."

"Oh I did! It was such a beautiful drive."

"Well... Welcome to Medicine Bow!" Karen exclaimed. "We're so excited to have you here!"

"Thank you! I am excited to be here and look forward

to seeing everything there is to see," she said with a laugh.

"It won't take you very long," said Karen. "Medicine Bow is a small community with less than 300 people but we love it here. I'm hoping you will like it enough to relocate. We really need a Veterinarian in our town!"

"I'd like to look things over and see what kind of housing is available. What I would like to find is a house large enough for us to live and also have the clinic there."

"That's a great idea. I might know just the perfect place for you."

"Great! I'd love to see it."

"I can tell you where it's located, and you can go look at it. It's at 613 Oregon Street. It is across highway #487 from here. A lady I know had a fourplex of apartments that she converted into one apartment and another huge one. I believe that would work."

"Thanks, Karen! I'll drive over there and look at it. If I'm interested maybe you can contact your friend."

"Sure, I'd be glad to."

"Thanks Karen! I'll let you know what I decide." Miranda left and drove to Oregon Street. She found the apartments and thought the huge one would be good for her. It should allow plenty of room for their living space plus room for her clinic. She would see about renting for now and if she stayed she might approach her landlord later about buying it. She didn't waste much time looking since she was unable to see the inside. She drove back to the Town Hall to see Karen. As she walked in the door she excitedly said, "I like it!"

"Great!" exclaimed Karen smiling. "Shall I call my friend?"

"Please do. I would love to see the inside."

"Give me your cell number and I will call you tonight after I talk to her."

"Thanks," she said as she gave her the phone number.

Miranda left and went back to the Virginian Hotel. She wanted to call home and check on Taylor and the family. "Sallie, it's Miranda. How are things going?"

"Everything is well," replied Sallie. "How's Medicine Bow? Do you like it there?"

"Matter of fact I think we're going to LOVE living here!"

"I hear excitement in your voice."

"Yes, I am excited! I feel as if this is where I am supposed to be. I think this town needs me."

"I'm sure they do and I know you will make them a great Veterinarian."

"Thanks Sallie, I will try my best. I have to go now; I just wanted to check on everyone back home."

"Don't worry about us. Take care of yourself and have a safe trip back home next week."

"See you soon. I will call again tomorrow. Bye for now."

"Bye, Miranda."

Miranda decided to go sightseeing a little. She saw the red roof of the Medicine Bow Museum and thought she would stop in there. As she walked in the door a lovely woman came to greet her. "Hello, and welcome to the Medicine Bow Museum. My name is Natalia and I'm the Director."

Miranda extended her hand and said, "I'm Miranda Sterling. It's very nice to meet you Natalia. What a lovely name! I don't think I have heard it before. I'm curious... what does it mean?"

Natalia laughed and replied, "It means 'Born at Christmas'."

"That's interesting! Were you born at Christmas?"

"Actually I was born in December, just not Christmas Day. So...how may I help you Ms. Sterling?"

"Oh it's Miranda to you."

"Okay Miranda. How may I be of service to you?"

"I'd just like to look around. I love museums."

"Go ahead and if I can help just let me know."

"Thanks," said Miranda as she walked down the aisle looking at the artifacts which consisted of items about Ranching, Union Pacific, Lincoln Highway, Wind Energy, Owen Wister's Cabin and Book. She browsed around for quite awhile then went back to talk to Natalia. "It's all very interesting."

"Thank you," said Natalia. "I really do enjoy working here. We are only open from Memorial Day through Labor Day."

"Why is that?" asked Miranda.

"We have early winters here. Sometimes we have such blowing snows that the roads are closed for a day or two."

"That's hard to imagine. Of course we have rough winters in Montana too."

"We certainly are happy to have you here in Medicine Bow! Hope you like it enough to relocate here."

"I am strongly thinking about it," laughed Miranda.

"It sure would be nice to have our very own Veterinarian. I have a dog and sometimes it's hard to find time to go into Laramie or Rawlins."

"Maybe you won't have to do that too much longer."

"I hope not," said Natalia with a smile.

"It was nice to meet you Natalia."

"Nice to meet you as well. Thanks for stopping by!"

Miranda left and went to the diner to eat a bite before returning to the hotel. Madison was still working and smiled at her as she entered the diner. Almost as soon as Miranda seated herself, Madison appeared with the menu. "Hello," she said with a smile.

"Hello, Madison. I think I would like a salad with Italian dressing for dinner."

"Coming right up." She left and returned in about fifteen minutes. Miranda enjoyed the salad and ate slowly while taking in the incredible view of the mountains. It would soon be dark. She hoped to hear from Karen tonight or in the morning. She was so anxious to see the apartment and determine if it would be suitable for living as well as a clinic.

She had been back at the hotel for about thirty minutes when her cell phone rang. It was Karen. The owner of the property could come to Medicine Bow day after tomorrow. Karen sounded almost as excited as Miranda. They talked a while then Miranda thanked her and they hung up. She decided to go to bed after she called home. Everything was fine there according to Sallie. That relieved Miranda's mind. Sleep came easily for her that night. She was more tired than she realized. She woke up the next morning feeling refreshed and ready for another day of exploring the town. She spent the day browsing around and talking to several people. This was such a friendly town. She knew she was going to love it here.

Today she was meeting with the property owner. She was excited! She drove out there at 1:00 p.m. A new Mercedes sat in front of the building. As she pulled up an attractive lady got out of the car. Miranda parked her car, got out and walked over to the other car. "Miranda?" asked the lady.

"Yes I'm Miranda Sterling."

"I'm Kate Robertson. I'm so happy to meet you Miranda!"

"Nice to meet you too, Kate!"

"Karen tells me you are interested in some of my property."

"That's correct. I need a place large enough for my daughter, her nanny and myself, as well as my Veterinarian Clinic."

"I think I have the perfect place for you."

"I have looked at the building and was so anxious to see inside."

"Well then what are we waiting for?" she laughed as the two of them walked toward the building.

They went through every room and Miranda carefully examined each detail. Her mind was turning as she looked. She was thinking about how to fit everything into this apartment. It was large and she could see no reason it wouldn't work. "I like it!" she told Kate. "I think it will be perfect."

"Great," expressed Kate. "When do you want to move? The apartment is available now."

"I have to get things settled at home and at my clinic. I have a doctor who wants to rent it so that will leave me free to come here. I think I could be here in two weeks. That will be the first of the month and that would be a good time."

"Sounds great to me!" exclaimed Kate. "I know the town must be excited!"

Miranda laughed, "They seem to be."

"I have a contract with me so we can get that part taken care of."

"Good, there's no use waiting."

"Thank you, Miranda. It's a pleasure doing business

with you," she said after Miranda had signed the contract. "I wish you well here in Medicine Bow."

Miranda was happy as they walked out the door. She decided to stop by the Town Hall and tell Karen, who was almost as excited as she was. They had known each other for only a few days and already there seemed to be a connection between them. Miranda was hoping they could become really good friends.

Chapter 5

Since Miranda had accomplished what she had set out to do, she decided to cut her visit short and go back home to Montana. She would leave in the morning. Since she would be back here in two weeks she needed as much time as possible to get things in order. She would be very busy getting her things together. She decided to rent a U-Haul and take everything at once. It would be easier that way. She would drive the truck and have Sallie drive her car taking Taylor with her.

She would have to buy new equipment for her clinic and find someone who could build what she needed. She was sure Karen would know someone. They never got that far in their conversation. It was getting close to nine o'clock and she decided to call Karen before going to bed.

"Hello," said a sweet voice.

"Karen, it's Miranda. I hate to bother you this late but I was wondering if you can help me."

"Sure, if I can."

"Do you know someone who can do some work for me? I need help on my clinic."

"Sure thing, I know the perfect man," she said with a laugh.

"Who is he?"

"His name is Jay Norton. He's a great guy and an excellent carpenter."

"That's great! Do you think you could talk to him while I'm gone and see if he would be interested in helping me?"

"Of course I will," replied Karen.

"Thank you so much Karen!"

"Anything for a friend! Have a safe trip tomorrow and I'll look forward to seeing you again in two weeks."

"Thanks, and I'll be anxious to get back."

Miranda went to bed shortly after talking to Karen. She had the best night she'd had in a long time. She was upbeat about the move and things seemed to be working out for her. Finally it seemed that she could put the past behind her and move on. She thanked the Lord for allowing her this opportunity. She knew He would help her if she would only let Him guide her life, and that is exactly what she intended to do.

She was up bright and early and looking forward to seeing her baby daughter later today. She sure had missed little Taylor and would be glad when they could get moved and be together again. She was also glad Sallie had agreed to come with them.

She had a safe drive home and everyone was excited to see her. Taylor jumped and squealed like her mommy had been gone for a month. A few days are a long time to a little one who is away from her mommy. It was good to see everyone too. Jennifer acted a little sad but Miranda told her she could come to visit often since it was only a five hour drive. She thought it would be good for Jennifer to get away from the ranch and visit with her also. She would love to have Gabe and the whole family if he could possibly get away. He was pretty much tied to the ranch since Mardi was gone.

The new Veterinarian, Dr. Bob Hartwell, came to see her the next night. He was very excited about renting her clinic. He had only been in practice for one year and worked with a clinic in Laurel. He was finally going to be his 'own' boss. He was engaged and was hoping with his new job he could finally afford to get married.

Miranda had done a background check on him and his record was squeaky clean. She knew she had to have him checked out since he would be working close to the house. In her mind she relived the kidnapping over and over. She didn't ever want her family to experience such grief again. One could never be too careful.

Dr. Hartwell moved into the clinic at the end of the week. He was thrilled beyond words, and kept thanking Miranda. She was happy for him. She felt good that she was giving him a new start in life and kept the rent as low as she possibly could. All she cared about was just enough to make the payment each month.

She had more things to concentrate on now...like what all she was going to take. She actually didn't have a lot of furniture, so she rented a medium size U-haul. Sallie was only taking her clothes and personal items which she could carry in Miranda's car.

At the end of the second week the U-haul was all loaded and ready to go. Miranda made sure to get an automatic truck. She could drive a straight, but didn't want to have to deal with that in the big truck. Sallie had the car loaded and they were ready to go. They left the ranch around nine o'clock Saturday morning after saying their sad goodbyes. Jennifer couldn't hold back the tears and that made Miranda cry. She had thought she would be strong...

They had an uneventful trip and arrived in Medicine Bow around four o'clock that afternoon. Miranda had called Karen with an estimated time of arrival so she had some guys there waiting to help unload the truck. Miranda was so thankful for the help. What would she do without her new friend Karen? She had taken her under her wing and had been the best friend a girl could ever have! She thanked God for Karen!

"Hello, Miranda! Welcome back!" exclaimed an excited Karen with a big grin.

"Thanks, Karen. I'm happy to be here, especially now that I have my daughter with me." They exchanged hugs like they had been apart for a year.

Sallie walked over to them with Taylor in her arms. Miranda introduced them to Karen. Taylor gave Karen a big smile then buried her head in Sallie's shoulder. She was a bit shy when she first met a stranger.

"Hello Sallie. Welcome to Medicine Bow," said Karen. "I hope you will like it here."

"Thanks Karen. I think I will."

"This little doll you're holding is such a cutie! I believe she looks like her mommy."

"She does," answered Sallie. "She's a lucky little girl seeing how beautiful her mommy is!"

"Yes, Miranda is beautiful," said Karen looking directly at Miranda. "Inside and out!"

"Thanks! I can say the same thing for you Karen! If we hadn't met I doubt very seriously that I would have moved here."

"Really?" asked Karen as a delightful smile crossed her face.

About two hours later the truck was unloaded and

the guys offered to deliver it into the next town tomorrow and save Miranda the trip. She was very grateful and paid them accordingly. They looked a little surprised when they saw the amount she gave them. Actually they would have done it for nothing, but she insisted they take the money.

"Miranda here is Jay's phone number. I told him you would call when you came back. I don't know how busy he is, so you probably should call and get your name in the pot."

"Thanks Karen. I will call him tonight."

Karen left shortly, so Miranda and Sallie unpacked a few boxes of the things they just had to have tonight. The rest could wait. About eight-thirty she decided to call Jay. He answered promptly and they had a nice conversation. He said he would be happy to do her work. He should be available in about a week. He was finishing up on a job and would be through in a few more days. That was fine with Miranda. That would give her time to get most of the things unpacked and put into place.

She called Jennifer after talking to Jay. "Things were quiet on the ranch," she said. She was missing Miranda more than she let on. Only time would take care of this.

Miranda went to bed about ten-thirty, and sleep came quickly. She dreamed she was back on the ranch and she couldn't find Mardi. Gabe had come in for supper and he thought Mardi was already in the house. Miranda went to the barn and called for him over and over. There was no answer...only silence. She roused in her sleep and realized it was a dream. The tears began to fall. She wept until her pillow was wet. She missed Mardi so much! Eventually she went back to sleep and the dream started all over again. This time she found him at the bottom of a steep cliff. He was covered in blood and his body was lifeless. She was trying to say, "There's no cliff on the ranch. Where is he?" But the words wouldn't come. She felt numb! She tried to move but couldn't. She screamed...Sallie came running into her room and shook her, "MIRANDA, WAKE UP!!!" shouted Sallie. "You're having a bad dream."

Miranda woke up and looked up at Sallie. "Where am I? Why are you here?" she asked.

"You're in Medicine Bow. You screamed and I came running. You scared me half to death!"

"I was dreaming about Mardi. It wasn't good, Sallie," she said sobbing. "He was dead and I found him at the bottom of a cliff. I couldn't figure out where he was."

"I am so sorry, Miranda!" Sallie hugged her as she cried.

"I hope I don't start having nightmares again."

"Me too! Let's pray together," suggested Sallie. So she knelt down by Miranda's bed and poured her heart out to God on behalf of her dear friend. Miranda slept the rest of the night with no more nightmares.

The next week flew by since Miranda and Sallie were so busy getting their new home straightened out. It was going to be a nice place. Miranda did need to go into another town and buy some furniture. That would have to wait a little while. Each of them had a bed so they could make do for now.

Chapter 6

One week later on a Monday morning Jay showed up at eight o'clock. Miranda had just gotten up. Sallie and Taylor were still asleep.

"Good Morning Dr. Sterling!" exclaimed a happy Jay. "Are you ready for me to start to work?"

"Of course, Jay! Sorry I'm still in my robe and I must look a fright."

"You look beautiful, Dr. Sterling."

"Please call me Miranda."

"Whatever you wish, Miranda."

"You can make a list of everything you need, and I will give you a check to buy it. I will also pay for your gas since you have a long distance to drive."

"Why thank you, Miranda. That is very thoughtful of you."

"I just don't want you spending your own money making trips for me."

"Thanks!"

Jay left and went to the downstairs part of the apartment where the clinic would be. He measured and figured out what he would need to get started. He made a list and went back upstairs to show Miranda a couple hours later. She had showered and was dressed by now. What a beautiful woman she is, he thought. Not only beautiful but sweet as well. Too bad he was already married he thought jokingly. No offense to his wife Carol. He loved her very much and she was a beautiful lady as well.

"I've made a list to get started. I am going to Home Depot in Casper. I have a large truck so I should be able to get everything I need to build the clinic. Of course all the equipment will have to be bought later."

"I understand. Thank you for doing this job for me. Since I don't know anyone it would have been hard for me to find a man willing to do this job. Thank God for my friend, Karen!"

"Oh, yes...Karen. She's a great girl! You're lucky to have her for a friend."

"I know!"

"She has not always lived in Medicine Bow you know!"

"Yes, I know. She told me she is from Pennsylvania. I imagine this is quite a change for her."

"Indeed it is! I am a native of Wyoming but I can imagine it would be hard to get used to. I guess you will have a story to tell after you have lived here awhile," he said with a laugh.

"I hope it's a good one."

"I think it will be. You are going to fit in just like you've always been here. The town is talking about how excited they are to finally have a Veterinarian Clinic here in Medicine Bow. They thought it would never happen."

"I am excited about it and look forward to working with all these wonderful people."

"Well I'd better get started on my way to Casper. It will take a couple hours to get there. I think I can set up an account at Home Depot and have them to send you the bill. That would be better than carrying a check."

"However you feel is best is fine with me. Be careful."

"See you later today," Jay said as he left. It was several hours later when he pulled in with a load of lumber. He was planning to get started in the morning. Miranda was excited.

As he promised, he and his friend were there by eight o'clock. They never wasted any time in getting started and worked continuously until lunch time. The left for one half hour and had lunch at the diner. Then it was back to work. Miranda was impressed how steady they worked. She couldn't wait to thank Karen for recommending them.

Week after week they worked. It was all falling into place. Miranda had to go into Casper to pick out the furniture and necessary tables she would need. Jay would go pick them up when the time came, which was less than three months. His work was finally done and he and Zane went to pick up Miranda's furniture order. It would take several more days to get everything into place. Then she would be ready to open up her practice. She had all necessary paperwork already done and was just waiting.

So four months after her move to Medicine Bow, she was ready to begin her work. She had a Grand Opening on Saturday with finger foods and drinks. She gave FREE dog biscuits for each customer who owned a dog. She had Kitty Treats for the owners of cats. It was a success. Everyone seemed so excited that she was ready to begin her work. Some of them made appointments with her for the following week.

Her new assistant, Jade Harper, was busy helping set up the appointments. Karen had recommended Jade to her. She only met her a month ago and took an instant liking to her. She thought they would work well together.

Jade was a cute, red headed, petite girl of twenty three who had just finished college and moved back to Medicine Bow. She was going to make a terrific assistant. Everything seemed to be falling into place.

Chapter 7

Social life in Medicine Bow was better than one would think. Someone was always inviting Miranda to a social event. Since the Community Hall had been renovated there was a lot of activity going on there. The next big event was 'WESTERN DAY'. Miranda was really looking forward to that. Coming from a ranch she knew exactly how to dress. The day finally got here and she was dressed in her best western wear. She didn't have to be told she looked stunning, she could feel it. They arrived at the Community Hall a few minutes late. Several people were already there and mostly the men were in groups talking. Sallie took Taylor and went inside with the ladies. Karen met Miranda and they were browsing around outside and having a general conversation. Both of them stopped talking and looked at each other. "Listen!" exclaimed Miranda.

Off in a distance they could hear the sound of the horse hooves hitting the pavement. As he approached Miranda could see that his wavy black hair lay gently up on his ears, nestled beneath his black, silver studded cowboy hat. A slight shadow of dark beard graced his tanned, chiseled face. He was ruggedly handsome which suggested that he spent a lot of time outdoors.

He was wearing a red and black plaid western shirt, black wranglers and black cowboy boots. He had the authentic cowboy look, Miranda noted. In fact he reminded her of Sam Elliott. Growing up she'd had a huge crush on Sam even though she knew she would never meet him. Watching this cowboy brought Sam back into her thoughts.

He dismounted his beautiful stallion which was as white as the pure driven snow. Miranda had never seen such a beautiful horse. There was nothing on their ranch that could compare to his beauty. She found herself staring at both the horse and the rider. He never seemed to notice her at all. There was something about him that she couldn't quite put her finger on. Somehow he seemed familiar. She knew that couldn't be true because there was so much distance between them. He proceeded to tie his horse to the hitching post and headed toward a group of men standing in front of the Community Hall. He never looked her way as he passed by. The men seemed to be in a deep discussion but stopped talking as he approached. He joined the group and was shaking hands with them so apparently they weren't strangers. He towered above the crowd. Miranda found that she just couldn't take her eyes off him. Who was this mysterious man? She really wanted to know...

After awhile he glanced around the crowd and his eyes stopped on Miranda. His eyes were icy cold like the color of blue steel. Miranda felt herself shiver. She had never seen such cold eyes in all her life. She glanced away for a few seconds then like a magnet was drawing her, she had to look back at him. He was still staring at her. She turned to her friend Karen, "Who is he?" she asked.

"His name is Elijah Warren, Eli for short. I really don't know much about him."

"Where did he come from? I've never seen him before."

"That's because he doesn't live in the town of Medicine Bow. He has a ranch south of here."

"Oh...does he come here often?" Miranda asked.

""A few times a year I think. He is always here for our Western Day Celebration."

"Does he always ride a horse?" asked Miranda with a chuckle.

"He does unless it's raining."

"Mmmm...Interesting! Is he married?"

"No but he was engaged once and two weeks before the wedding she told him she was in love with another man."

"Ouch! That's a tough one!"

"She was a beautiful blonde and looked somewhat like you," added Karen.

"So that's why he gave me such an icy stare?"

"Could be," replied Karen.

"I'm sorry I upset him. As you know I am innocent in this case."

"Of course you are Miranda. Just ignore him and don't let him spoil your day. We are so happy to have you living here in Medicine Bow. You are a great asset to our town."

"Thank you Karen. I am happy to be here. I am learning to love this little town."

"Good and don't you worry about Eli. He has been this way for the past few years. I think when he sees a beautiful blonde it brings back memories of his lost love, Serena."

"I didn't mean to upset him. I just didn't know...Has he never gotten over her?"

"I actually don't think he has."

"Does he ever date anyone?" asked Miranda curiously.

"If he does I don't know anything about it. He is a very private person anyway."

"He needs to stop living in the past and move on," said Miranda.

"Indeed he does! Have you thought about taking your own advice Miranda?"

Miranda thought for a moment and said, "I guess you're right Karen. I haven't even thought about dating since Mardi died. He was the love of my life! I don't think I could ever fall in love again."

"Never say never!"

"We'll see," said Miranda with a sigh. "For now I just want to concentrate on raising Taylor and my job."

"You're sure good at what you do," added Karen.

"Thank you!"

"Medicine Bow is so lucky, or should I say blessed that you moved here."

"Thanks! I feel that I made the right decision in moving here. Everyone has been so nice and supportive."

"Even though our town is small, we are a close knit community."

"I've noticed that and I am quite impressed. The fact that I was accepted so quickly says a lot about the town. They have made me feel so welcome and part of the community. I am really grateful for that!"

"You have fit in so well Miranda and we are so happy to have a Veterinarian in our town!"

"I'm happy to be here!"

Karen turned to Miranda and said, "Let's walk over there. I'd like for you to meet Eli."

"Meet Eli? I think I'm the last person he wants to meet!"

"Come on," urged Karen as she started walking toward the men.

Miranda followed her. When they were nearby, Eli turned his attention to them. "Hello Eli," said Karen. "Nice to see you today." Without smiling he returned her greeting. He shifted his gaze to Miranda and locked eyes with her. She had been right...he did have eyes of steel. She was feeling very uncomfortable as she shifted her weight. She wanted to turn and run.

"Eli I'd like for you to meet my good friend and the town's new Veterinarian Miranda Sterling," said Karen.

Without changing his facial expression he extended his hand and said, "Nice to meet you Dr. Sterling."

Miranda looked straight into those icy cold blue eyes and replied, "Nice to meet you too Mr. Warren."

"Why so formal?" asked Karen with a nervous laugh.

"Eli to you then," he remarked sarcastically. "So how do you like Medicine Bow?"

"Actually, I love it here," replied Miranda.

"So you're a Veterinarian?" he asked.

"Yes and I love working with animals. I find it more relaxing than being with humans," she said giving him that 'I mean you' look.

"Oh really? That's an interesting thought," he remarked.

"So what do you do?"

"I'm a rancher. I own a ranch south of here."

"That's nice. Actually I lived on a ranch before I moved here."

"Is that so?" he asked rolling his eyes. "Where might that be?"

"Montana. Our ranch is in Laurel."

"Oh I've heard of Laurel, Montana. In fact I have been there. Why did you leave your ranch to come here?"

"It's a long story," she said sadly with tears welling up in her eyes.

He could see the sadness in her eyes and decided not to pursue the issue. "Well anyway I'm sure the people of Medicine Bow are happy to have you here. I hope you will stay and not let them down. These are good people and don't deserve anything but the best. I hope you will be everything they need!"

"Absolutely I'll give it my best shot," she answered as she turned and walked away. She'd had enough of his arrogant ways. How dare he judge her because she was a blonde? Karen followed her inside the building where they joined the rest of the women who were preparing the tables. There was so much delicious looking food but somehow Miranda's appetite had diminished. She told herself she was not going to let that man ruin her day. She went over to the dessert table and dropped off her famous Chocolate-Caramel Cake. Then she went to the meat table and left her Golden Fried Chicken.

"I'm sorry, Miranda," said Karen.

"For what?"

"For the way Eli acted. He can be quite annoying, if you know what I mean."

"That's the feeling I got from him. It seems like he doesn't like me because I'm blonde. Does he treat all blondes this way? Are we all supposed to be dumb?"

"Just ignore him and don't give him another thought. Don't let him ruin your day."

"I'll try...but he got under my skin!" Miranda exclaimed.

"Everyone around here is used to him and the way

he acts. He hasn't always been like this. When Serena left him that's when he changed. Come on...I have some more people I would like for you to meet."

They walked over to another group of men and as Karen spoke, they all turned their attention to the two girls. "Hello Gentlemen."

"Hi Karen," said a nice looking man with a huge smile. "For those of you who haven't met her yet, I'd like to introduce you to our new town Veterinarian, Dr. Miranda Sterling."

The nice looking man stepped forward and extended his hand, "Hello Dr. Sterling. It's nice to meet you. I'm Ethan Kane... Sheriff of Carbon County."

"Hello Mr. Kane. It's a pleasure to meet you," she said with a smile.

"Call me Ethan. Everyone else does."

"Okay I'm glad to meet you ETHAN!"

He laughed and asked her how she likes living in Medicine Bow.

"I love it here."

"That's great! I know they are happy to have you."

"They tell me they are," she said with a laugh.

"I know this is blunt but are you married?"

"You don't waste any time do you? Actually I am a widow with a small daughter. My husband was accidently killed about two years ago."

"I'm so sorry to hear that!"

"Thank you. That's one of the reasons I am here. I had to get away from the place of the accident and all the bad memories."

"So you're making a new start?"

"I'm trying to."

"I wish you the best," he said apologetically.

"Thank you."

"Perhaps we'll meet again sometime," said Ethan with a smile.

"Perhaps we will."

He rejoined the group of men he had been talking to so Miranda and Karen left. Karen led her to another group of men. "I have someone else I want you to meet."

"Karen, are you trying to play matchmaker?" she asked with a laugh.

"I'm just introducing you...the rest is up to you!"

"Hello Guys," said Karen as they approached the group. She singled out a medium height, muscled man with the look of Sean Connery. He was all smiles as Karen introduced him to Miranda. "Morgan I'd like for you to meet Dr. Miranda Sterling."

He extended his hand to her and said, "So nice to meet you Dr. Sterling. I'm Morgan Cole. I've been hearing some good things about you!"

"Thank you, Morgan. Just call me Miranda."

"Okay Miranda and welcome to Medicine Bow! I hope our paths will cross again sometime."

"Do you live in Medicine Bow?"

"No I live in Casper. That's about ninety-five miles from here. I own a motorcycle shop called Morgan Harley Davidson."

"Oh that's interesting. You had quite a drive today."

"A couple hours but I didn't mind since I rode my bike."

"Sounds like fun! I've always been intrigued by motorcycles especially a Harley."

"Well you're in luck! My shop is filled with Harley bikes. Maybe you would like to go for a ride sometime."

"Wow! That sounds like an invitation too good to turn down!"

"Then is it a date?" he asked.

"When?"

"Soon," he promised. "If you'll give me your phone number I will call you."

So she gave him one of her business cards along with a smile. She was excited! This would be her first date since Mardi died. She felt a little guilty even though she was excited. She knew Mardi would want her to go on with her life and not grieve for him forever. It seemed that things were turning around for her. She had grieved so hard and so long for Mardi. She had been praying for God's will to be done in her life, so if He wanted her to be happy again He would supply the perfect man. She prayed she would not judge every man by Mardi. He had been the love of her life. She knew little Taylor needed a 'daddy' and she had to make sure if she ever remarried that he would be good to her child. Not all men are cut out to be a daddy. It would take a very special man to be a daddy to someone else's child. She was trusting God to work it all out and supply that perfect man if that was His will for her.

"Wow," said Karen after they said goodbye to Morgan and walked in another direction. "YOU HAVE A DATE! I am so excited for you!"

"Thanks Karen! It happened so quickly I hardly knew what was happening!"

"That's the best way," she laughed.

"He may not even call."

"I just bet he will."

"We'll see," said Miranda with a sigh.

Chapter 8

A week later when she was least expecting it, her phone rang. She didn't recognize the number but answered it anyway. "Hello Sterling residence."

"Miranda?" asked a male voice.

"Yes this is Miranda. How may I help you?"

"It's Morgan...Morgan Cole...the Harley guy you promised to go out with."

She could hear him laughing as he talked. "Hello Morgan. Nice to hear from you."

"How have you been? Have you gotten settled in yet?"

"We're trying. I still have some boxes to unpack. It seems like it always takes so long."

"Sounds like you need some fun in your life," he said with a chuckle.

"Maybe I do. What would you suggest?"

"How about a ride on my Harley?"

"Sounds like fun!" she exclaimed. "When?"

"How about this Saturday? Will you be free then?"

"That should be fine. I'm blessed to have a built-in babysitter."

"Indeed you are!"

"How about noon on Saturday? We'll go to the diner and grab a bite to eat before we ride."

"Sounds great to me!"

He could hear the excitement in her voice. "Great! I'll see you then!"

They hung up the phone and Miranda ran to tell Sallie who was very excited for her. "I am so happy for you Miranda. It's about time you start living again."

"What about you Sallie? Have you ever thought of trying to find love again?"

"Not really. Bobby is the love of my life. He always has been and always will be. There is no other man who could ever take his place."

"Never say never my friend!"

"I'm afraid it will be NEVER for me!"

"If you feel this way then I won't have to worry about losing you will I?"

"I guess you won't."

"So no matter where we might live you will always go with us right?"

"If you want me to I will," answered Sallie.

"We do! You are more than a nanny to Taylor. You are more like the Grandmother she never knew."

Sallie smiled and replied, "I couldn't love her any more than I already do if she was my real Granddaughter!"

"She loves you, too! You know that I love you also!"

"I know," said Sallie with a smile. "I love you too, Miranda! I guess I will be with you as long as I live. I have given up hope of ever having Bobby again. I thought when he first left that he might come back to me someday but I doubt that ever happens. It's been too long..."

"I'm so sorry, Sallie! I wish you hadn't gone through this painful experience. Just trust the Lord and He will see you through. There is a brighter day ahead. If not in this world...then in the world to come."

"I know and I have been trusting the Lord, Miranda. I don't think I could have made it if it hadn't been for Him! He gives me peace and comfort when no one else can. I am looking forward to the day when I can go be with Him!"

"I know and that is a wonderful thought. I think about it too! My dad and mother are both with Him, and I long to see them again."

"I know that will be a happy reunion for you."

"Yes, it will be!" exclaimed Miranda. "Now... How do you feel about a day out today? I need to go to Cheyenne and do some shopping. I'd like to get a new pair of jeans and maybe a black leather jacket for my motorcycle ride on Saturday. If I'm going to be a Harley Chick I need to dress the part," she said laughing.

"Sounds great! A day out will do all of us good. Take all the time you need to get ready and I will take care of Taylor."

"Thanks, Sallie...I don't know what I would do without you!"

"Don't even think about it. I will be here for you as long as you need me."

"Sounds wonderful to me!"

They had a wonderful drive into Cheyenne. It was a beautiful view along the way. They went to the mall and did some shopping. Miranda found a leather shop and bought a black leather jacket. It was exactly what she was looking for. Then she went to a department store and got a couple pairs of jeans. She did some shopping for Taylor and also bought Sallie an outfit. They went to a nice restaurant for lunch and finished the rest of their shopping afterward. It was a long but enjoyable day. Taylor slept all the way home.

Saturday was here and it was her big day. She got up in a very good mood and was singing softly as she was preparing breakfast for the three of them. Sallie had just brought Taylor into the kitchen.

"Is there something I can do?" asked Sallie.

"Not really as I am almost finished," replied Miranda with a big smile.

"You seem to be in a good mood this morning. I wonder why..."

"I guess I am excited about going out with Morgan. I'm looking forward to the motorcycle ride."

"Just be careful."

"I'm sure Morgan is a good rider. He's been riding for years."

They ate breakfast and Sallie told Miranda she would clean up the kitchen. She insisted that Miranda go on and get ready for her date. It was already nine o'clock. So Miranda did as Sallie suggested and headed for the shower. Two hours later she was dressed ready to go. She was wearing her new jeans with a red turtleneck sweater and silver jewelry. Her long golden hair was flowing down her back. She didn't realize how beautiful she was.

"You look stunning!" exclaimed Sallie. "You're surely going to make Morgan fall in love with you!"

"Oh, Sallie...this is only our first date. Besides, I'm not trying to make Morgan or anyone else fall in love with me. That's the last thing I need."

"Now Miranda you know you're too young to spend the rest of your life alone!"

"Maybe...but I don't want to think about that now."

At ten minutes before noon they could hear the sound of a motorcycle approaching. Miranda glanced out the window just as he pulled into the driveway. He was dressed completely in black. She loved that look! THE MAN IN

BLACK! Morgan dismounted, pulled off his helmet and headed for the door. Miranda waited for him to ring the doorbell. She didn't want to appear overanxious. She opened the door after the second ring. "Hello Morgan," she pleasantly said. "Come in. Did you have a nice ride?"

"Hi Miranda, and yes I had a great trip. I always enjoy riding, though. By the way, you look beautiful!" he exclaimed with a big smile as he stepped inside.

"Thank you," she replied. "I would like for you to meet my daughter and her nanny." Sallie and Taylor had just entered the room.

"Morgan, this is my daughter, Taylor, and her wonderful nanny Sallie."

"Nice to meet you both," he said as he shook hands with Sallie and stooped down to Taylor's level. He said a few words to her before rising to his feet. She was shy and hid behind Sallie.

"Are you ready to hit the road?" he asked Miranda.

"Sure," she replied. She kissed Taylor and told her to be a good girl. They said their goodbyes and Miranda walked out the door that Morgan was holding open for her.

"Have your ridden before?" he asked.

"No, this is my first time."

"You're in for a treat!"

"I'm excited about it. I have always wanted to go for a ride on a motorcycle. I am an accomplished horse rider though. Have you ever ridden a horse?"

"I'm afraid not. That's not my thing. I'll just stick to the bike."

"I guess both can be exciting although I don't think I could ever ride a bike alone."

"I'm sure you could but it takes a lot of practice. The hardest thing for women is learning to hold the bike upright. I've seem too many lay it over," he laughed.

"Well I wouldn't want to be ONE of them! I'll just stick to being doubled."

Morgan gave her a helmet and told her to put it on. She did and it felt so weird and heavy. She climbed on behind him and he started the motor. This sure is loud, she thought. She had heard that a Harley was the loudest of all bikes. She never said a word about it. He turned around in the driveway and off they went. He was going slow much to her liking. She was hoping he wouldn't go too fast. They drove over to the diner and went in to have lunch. They were met by a smiling Madison.

"Hello," she said smiling at Miranda and raising her eyebrows. "Who's your new friend?"

"Oh, Madison, this is Morgan Cole."

"New around here?" she asked looking directly at him.

"You might say that. I'm from Casper, although I do grace Medicine Bow every now and then."

"I don't remember seeing you before," said Madison.

"Maybe you weren't looking for me," he teased.

She blushed and handed them menus. "I'll be back in a few minutes to take your order."

"Thanks," she looked at Morgan and laughed. "I do believe Madison thought you were cute. Did you see her blush?"

"I saw her. She is so young. She'll get over it one day." Changing the subject he asked, "What would you like to eat?"

"I feel like having a burger and fries along with iced tea."

"Sounds good to me. I'll order for both of us if that's okay with you."

"That's great...go ahead. I like a 'take charge' man!"

Morgan ordered when Madison came back. She

brought their food in less than twenty minutes. Everything was hot and very delicious.

Half an hour later they were on the Harley again. This time they headed for open country. Miranda had never been on the road Morgan took her. They rode south about ten miles and came upon a ranch. She remembered Eli Warren saying he had a ranch ten miles south of Medicine Bow. Could this be it? She would never ask Morgan. Wait! She just saw a tall man emerge from the house. Is this him? Could it possibly be him she wondered. She only got a glimpse of him as they passed by so quickly. This made her heart beat faster...Forget him she told herself. He has too much baggage. Besides here she was with Morgan and she needed to give him all her attention. She tried to put Eli out of her mind but there was just something about him that kept her from forgetting.

"Are you having fun?" asked Morgan as he turned his head sideways to see her.

"Yes, I'm having a lot of fun!" She meant it. She was thoroughly enjoying her first motorcycle ride. Morgan had noticed her black leather jacket and had commented on it as soon as she put it on back at the house. She never let on that it was new. Girls need not tell all they know.

They rode for another three hours seeing country that Miranda had never seen before. She soaked in all the beauty all around her. In her mind she had no doubt this was where she belonged. This was her destiny.

It was almost dinner time when they got back to Medicine Bow. She invited Morgan in but since he had another couple hours to ride he felt he should be going. "Thank you so much for a wonderful day!" she said sweetly.

"Thank you!" he exclaimed. "I don't think I've ever had a more beautiful passenger on my bike!"

"Thanks! You are too kind! I really did enjoy riding with you."

"Let's do it again soon," he suggested.

"Sounds good to me."

"How about in two weeks? I already have something scheduled for next weekend."

"That will be fine. I'll look forward to it. Have a safe ride back to Casper."

"I'll call you," he said just before he started the motor again. She waved to him as he went out the driveway.

She was met by Sallie and Taylor as soon as she entered the house. "So how was your day?" asked an anxious Sallie.

"Actually it was great!"

"I'm happy to hear that. Taylor and I had a good day also. I fixed a picnic and we went out in the back yard and ate. She had so much fun."

"That's good."

"Tell me about Morgan. Do you like him well enough to go out with him again?"

"Yes I do, and we have another date in two weeks."

"Two weeks?"

"Yes, he already had a commitment for next Saturday."

"Do you suppose it's another girl?" asked Sallie.

"I don't know. It really doesn't matter. I'm sure he's had more than his share of women. With his good looks and that muscled body, who could resist him?"

"I'd take it slow if I were you Miranda."

"Oh don't worry, Sallie. I'm certainly not in love and doubt if I ever will be."

"I think you should date several guys before thinking about settling down. You want to make sure you find the right one for you."

"That's exactly how I feel. I am not rushing into anything! For now I just want to date and have fun."

"I'm glad to hear that. You know I worry about you like you were my daughter. I guess you are the daughter I never had," she said smiling.

Chapter 9

Several days later Miranda received a surprise call from Morgan. She wasn't expecting to hear from him until maybe the night before their date. "Hello Miranda," he said when she answered the phone. "How are things going with you?"

"Going well, thank you. It's nice to hear from you."

"Are you surprised?"

"Actually I am!"

"I need a favor. Do you think you can help me?"

"Help you with what?" she asked laughing.

"I have a friend, Johnathan Carter, who also loves to ride. I told him about our date and he was wondering if you have a friend who might be interested in riding with him. If you do, we could all ride together."

"Let me think...since I am new here and don't know many people yet, the only one I know would be my friend, Karen Heath. I will talk to her and let you know."

"Sounds good. Have a good day."

"Thanks. Same to you!"

Miranda called Karen immediately after her conversation with Morgan. "Hi Karen."

"Hello, Miranda. What are you doing today?"

"Not much. I just had an unexpected call from Morgan."

"Really? What did he want?"

"He wanted me to do him a favor. It seems he has a friend who is looking for a date and I told him about you."

"YOU DID WHAT?"

"I told him you were available," laughed Miranda.

"Who is this guy?"

"His name is Johnathan Carter. He is a biker also."

"I'm not so sure about that. I'm not really into bikers."

"I didn't think I was either but I really did enjoy riding with Morgan. It is a feeling unlike any I have ever experienced. Riding against the wind is such a wonderful feeling of being free. Please say you will go! We are going to double date."

"Well in that case, I guess I will go. I have never ridden a motorcycle. Actually no one ever asked me before."

"Thanks, Karen. I don't think you will regret it. We will have a great time!"

"If you say so," added Karen.

Karen decided to come to Miranda's house that Saturday morning. If she didn't like Johnathan at least he wouldn't know where she lives. She got there about thirty minutes before they came rolling into the driveway. "Wow! They sure are loud!" exclaimed Karen.

"You'll get used to it. I did!"

The guys came strolling up to the door and rang the doorbell. Miranda cheerfully opened the door. "Good Morning, Guys!"

"Good Morning to you!" exclaimed Morgan. "I'd like for you to meet Johnathan Carter."

"Hi Johnathan," said Miranda. "It's so nice to meet you, and this is my friend Karen Heath."

Karen extended her hand and said, "Nice to meet you, Johnathan."

"Likewise," said Johnathan. "Are you ready for a bike ride?"

"I guess," she said.

"Have you ridden before?"

"No, this will be my first time and I must admit I am a little nervous."

"You'll be fine. I'll take good care of you," he said giving her a reassuring smile.

"Thanks."

They said goodbye to Sallie and Taylor and left.

The guys took them to a very nice restaurant for lunch. By now they were all starving. The food was delicious and they ate until they were miserable. Morgan stood up and rubbed his stomach. "Oooh...I ate too much!" he exclaimed. He sat back down and asked if they wanted dessert.

"None for me," replied Miranda.

"Me neither," said Karen. "I don't think I could hold another bite of anything."

Johnathan looked over at Karen and asked, "So Karen, where do you work?"

"I am the Town Clerk/Treasurer for the town of Medicine Bow. I have lots of other duties also."

"Sounds like a good job."

"It really is...I love my job!"

"That's great. It always helps it you like your job."

"What do you do?" she asked.

"I'm a Firefighter."

"Oh, I admire firefighters, but it is a dangerous job."

"Everything can be dangerous. The way I look at it you are not going until God says it's your time."

"That's very true. I believe that also."

"Are you girls ready to go?" asked Morgan.

"I'm ready," said Miranda.

"Me too," added Karen.

They went outside and got on the motorcycles and left. The girls had no idea where they were going. They were just enjoying the ride. They rode for a couple hours and reached the town of Casper.

"I know I brought you here two weeks ago, Miranda, but Johnathan wanted to show Karen where he lives."

"That's fine with me. I just enjoy riding." She had been surprised when Morgan showed her where he lived. Everything was clean and in order. She wondered if he had a maid or if he was just a good housekeeper.

They went to Johnathan's house and rested for a short while then hit the road again. It was getting late by the time they got back to Medicine Bow. The guys left after dropping them off at Miranda's place.

"Well, what do you think of Johnathan?" asked Miranda.

"I think he is wonderful and very cute," replied Karen with a smile. "I sure hope he will ask me out again."

"He seemed to be smitten with you so I don't think you have anything to worry about."

"I hope not! How do you feel about Morgan?"

"I like Morgan a lot and enjoy his company, but I can't see a future with him. I think we are too different. For now I am just enjoying myself. I have no plans for settling down anytime soon."

Karen left and Miranda went into her house. Again she was met by Sallie and Taylor, who was very excited to see her Mommy.

"Miranda, you had a call while you were gone. He said his name was Ethan Kane and that he would call back tonight. He didn't want to leave a message."

"Ethan Kane...oh I met him on Western Day. He is the Sheriff of Carbon County. I wonder what he wants."

"I guess you'll find out soon."

Sallie had dinner ready and after they ate Miranda told her she would do the dishes. Before she finished the phone rang. Sallie answered and brought the phone to Miranda. "Hello, Miranda speaking."

"Miranda, it's Ethan Kane. Remember me?"

"Of course I remember you! How are you?"

"I'm doing well and hopefully I'll be doing even better if you will let me take you to dinner one night soon."

Caught off guard Miranda remained silent.

"Are you still there Miranda?" he asked in apprehension.

"I'm here. I'm just surprised I guess."

"Why would that be?" he asked with a nervous laugh.

"I guess I never dreamed you were interested in me. Karen said you are very busy and don't have much time for a social life."

"That is very true. Sometimes I just need a diversion."

"Is that what I am?" she asked laughing.

"That's not what I meant."

"Well what DID you mean?"

"Seriously, I would love to take you to dinner. I am off tomorrow. I know this is a short notice, but could you possibly go then?"

"I don't have anything planned for the afternoon. Of course we go to church in the morning."

"That's good. Everyone should go to church. May I pick you up around five o'clock?"

"That sounds good. I'll see you then."

When Miranda got off the phone she went to find Sallie. "You are not going to believe this. I have a dinner date with Ethan Kane tomorrow evening."

"You what?"

"He wants to take me to dinner."

"What about Morgan?"

"What about him? I'm not looking for someone to marry. I think I should date different guys and maybe somewhere along the way I may meet MR. RIGHT."

"You know this could get complicated!"

"I'll manage," laughed Miranda.

Chapter 10

Sunday after church Miranda spent an hour looking through her closet and trying on outfits. She wanted to look her very best for her date with Ethan later today. She finally settled on black pants and an emerald green silk blouse with ruffles. She knew that green was her best color and brought out the green in her eyes. It also looked good with her long golden hair.

A few minutes before five o'clock Ethan pulled in at her house. She peeped out the window and liked what she saw. He was wearing dark navy dress pants and a light blue dress shirt. His sandy colored hair was styled perfectly. He reminded her of Robert Redford.

Miranda met him at the door. "Come in."

Sallie and Taylor had just walked into the room as he came through the front door. "Ethan, I would like for you to meet my daughter, Taylor, and her nanny Sallie."

"Hello, Taylor and Sallie. Nice to meet you." He bent down and talked to Taylor. For some reason she wasn't as shy with him as she had been with Morgan.

"We'll be back later Sallie," said Miranda as they were walking out the door.

"Have fun."

"Thanks."

Ethan took her to Luciano's, an Italian restaurant for a romantic dinner. She wasn't sure she was ready for this. They had driven to Laramie to eat. Talk was minimal on the way. There didn't seem to be a need for words. She was really happy he had asked her out. He was completely different from Morgan, who was just a big boy at heart.

She was having more fun since she moved to Medicine Bow. Having Sallie to take care of Taylor allowed her to enjoy dating. She didn't intend to get serious with anyone. Dinner was nice and the company even nicer. Ethan was more serious and even Miranda's personality was different when she was with him. That made her wonder...how she could be so different with the two men.

The drive back home was nice. She lay her head back and was in deep thought when the sound of his voice interrupted her thought. "Are you okay?" he asked. "You are really quiet."

"I'm fine... just thinking," she replied.

"About me, I hope."

"Actually I was thinking about you and us."

"Good, I like the sound of US."

"We'll just have to wait and see where this takes us," Miranda said with a smile.

"I hope it takes us to the altar."

"You are really jumping forward, aren't you?"

"It never hurts for a man to dream."

"I thought only women do that."

"Some men dream too, you know."

"I thought you were a hard nose cop!" she laughed.

"I am that by day and a romantic by night."

"Oh I like the sound of that!" she exclaimed.

When they got to her house he cut off the engine. "Do

you care if I come in for a few minutes? There is something I would like to ask you."

"Sure, you are welcome to come in."

"Good," he said with relief.

They walked in the house and sat down on the couch. "Would you like a cup of coffee?" she asked.

"Yes, that would be great."

Miranda went into the kitchen and poured two cups of coffee. Sallie always kept coffee made. She came back and handed him the coffee and sat down beside him. "Now what is this you want to talk to me about?"

"I know this is our first date but there is something different about you from any other girl I have dated. I can see a future for us. How do you feel about that?"

"It's possible I think. I had a great time with you tonight. Thank you very much for the wonderful meal and pleasant company."

"I was honored to take you out!" he exclaimed. "I can't wait to take you out again. I will have to check my schedule and see when I'm off duty again. I will call you."

"That sounds great."

"I'll be going now. I have a long drive. I'll call you soon."

"Okay, and thanks again for a lovely evening."

"You're welcome," he replied as he walked out the door.

"WOW, this is going too fast," said Miranda out loud after he had gone. She knew she couldn't let him think she was going to marry him, at least not yet. It would take time for her to decide if this was right for her. She was not going to let him rush her into anything. She got ready for bed but sleep evaded her. She had too much on her mind. "This is not good," she said aloud. "I just cannot do this!" Finally sleep came and she remembered thinking just before she dropped off to sleep that MEN certainly can complicate a woman's life.

The next morning Sallie asked her about her date. "I had fun but I think he wants more than just dating. He was talking about our future."

"Your future? Please don't let him rush you into anything that you may regret later. That's just a word of advice from an old lady."

Miranda hugged her and thanked her for her concern. "I am going to take it slow, I promise."

"I'm glad to hear that."

The phone rang while they were still at the table. It was Ethan. It seemed he had next Saturday and Sunday off. "Can we go out Saturday?"

Thinking that Saturday was the day she and Morgan usually dated she asked, "How about Sunday? That would be better for me."

"Sunday it is then. I'll see you around five o'clock. Have a good week. If I get a chance I may call you before then."

"Good. I'll see you Sunday." He did call her that week... three times. She was surprised and happy although she was a little worried. She was afraid he was reading more into this relationship than was actually there. She was determined to take it slow. She was not ready to settle down...it was too soon!

Morgan called her Thursday night to see if she was free on Saturday. They made a date for a picnic lunch at the town park. She was looking forward to seeing him again. She knew she would be comparing the two guys. Of course they would never know it. She was beginning to wonder if Sallie may be right. Maybe dating two men might be more than she could handle. Sooner or later they would find out about each other and she could possibly lose both of them. She was at the point of not knowing what to do. She liked both of them and it would be hard to choose. Morgan was carefree and fun. Ethan was more family oriented. Which suited her best? She knew one day she would have to choose. But for now she was having fun and decided to keep dating both men as long as she could juggle the dates.

Karen and Johnathan were hitting it off really well. Things seemed to be going very well for them. Karen was in Heaven. Miranda saw such a change in her since she had started dating Johnathan. Miranda was happy for her Best Friend.

Chapter 11

Monday morning came and Miranda was back at work. Around ten o'clock a man walked into the clinic carrying a rather large dog which appeared to be an English Shepherd. Jade was sitting at the front desk when he arrived. "How may I help you?" she asked looking at the dog.

"I need to see Dr. Sterling," he replied. "My dog is very ill."

"I'm so sorry," said Jade. "Please have a seat and Dr. Sterling will be with you shortly." Jade left and went back to tell Miranda.

"Tell him to bring his dog on back."

Jade went back into the waiting room and told him that Dr. Sterling would see him now. He got up once again holding on to his beloved dog and followed Jade.

"Good Morning," said Miranda and then realized who she was speaking to. "Mr. Warren...what can I do for you today?"

"My dog, Hero, is very sick. He refuses to eat and just seems lifeless."

"How long has he been this way?"

"Two days. I usually take him to another town but since you are closer I thought I would bring him here."

He laid the dog on the table and Miranda started to examine him. His heartbeat was faint and his lungs didn't sound good. He was breathing hard. "How old is this dog?" she asked.

"He's ten years old."

"I think he has cancer in his lungs and they are filling with fluid. I can do a test to make sure."

"That's okay I believe you. Is there anything you can do for him?"

"I don't think so. I can either put him to sleep or you can take him home and let him die there. I don't think it will be very long. You can save him from suffering if we put him to sleep."

"As much as I hate to do that I know you're right. So go ahead and do what you have to do. I do want to take him back to the ranch and bury him. He has been such a faithful companion and I want him to rest near the house. He saved my life one time but that's another story."

"I understand," replied Miranda with tears in her eyes. She went to prepare a shot and administered it to the dog. He died instantly. "I'm very sorry, Mr. Warren." She looked him directly in the eyes and saw the tears start and roll down his face.

"Thank you and call me Eli," he said as he wiped the tears with his suntanned hands.

"Okay, Eli."

Miranda wrapped Hero in a sheet then put him in a box and handed him to Eli. "Are you going to be okay?" she asked him.

"I'll be okay. I'll just have to get used to not having him around. He was like my shadow."

"I know how attached you can get to dogs. When I

lived on Prince Edward Island I had six Siberian Husky dogs and I loved them so much."

"What happened to them?"

"When I moved back to Montana my brother bought my house and he kept the dogs. I miss them so much!"

"That sounds like an interesting story. I'd like to hear it sometime. Maybe you could come out to the ranch sometime and tell me your story. I would love to hear it."

"Perhaps I can. I do have a story to tell and plenty of tragedy to go along with it," she added and gave him a smile.

"Thank you for being so caring with Hero. It means a lot to me!"

He walked out the door and stopped to pay Jade. "There is no charge," said Jade.

"What? I don't expect charity!"

"It's not charity, Mr. Warren. Dr. Sterling is doing a neighborly thing."

"In that case thank you." He walked out to his truck and loaded Hero for his final ride. As he drove home he thought about that beautiful doctor of animals. She was beautiful on the inside as well. He would like to get to know her better. He wasn't sure what the right approach was. He was certain she would be dating someone already. He would have to find out. Maybe he could call Karen at the Town Hall and find out since she seemed to be a good friend of the doctor.

That's what he did the very next day. He happened to catch her when she wasn't busy. He was anxious to know more about Miranda. "Karen, this is Eli Warren. How are you today?"

"I'm doing well thank you, and I am so sorry to hear about your dog!"

"Thanks Karen. I was wondering if you can help me. I

would like to know more about Dr. Sterling. I have never met anyone like her before."

"You're not falling for her are you?" she asked teasingly.

"No, I just want to know more about her. Is she dating anyone?"

"I'm afraid she is. In fact, she is dating two men at the present."

"TWO?" he asked as if he was stunned.

"Well yes...she is not ready to get married and didn't want to settle down with one guy. She's had so much tragedy in her life and she is taking it slow."

"Me of all people can understand that. I don't think I could date two women at one time though. I'm afraid I would get mixed up and make a date with both of them for the same night," he laughed.

"That certainly could happen. I told Miranda she should be careful."

"May I ask the names of the guys she is dating?"

"Morgan Cole from Casper. He owns a Harley Motorcycle Shop. The other one is the Sheriff of Carbon County. I'm sure you know Ethan Kane."

"Sure I know Ethan. He's a fine man and may I add a very lucky one too!"

"I think so too. I'm not sure which one she likes best."

"How about you, are you dating anyone?"

"Yes, I'm dating Johnathan Carter. He's from Casper also and friends with Morgan. In fact that is how I met this wonderful Firefighter!"

"Sounds like it is serious."

"I hope so. I am totally in love with this man!"

"That's great! I am very happy for you."

"Listen, as a friend, please don't mention to Miranda that I asked about her."

"As you wish, Eli. Your secret is safe with me."

"Thanks and maybe I'll be back in Medicine Bow soon."

"Any time."

Eli was glad he got to talk to Karen. He was disappointed that Miranda was dating not one but two men. Or maybe that could be a good thing. As long as she was dating both that meant she was not thinking of marriage.

He decided it would be best to forget about Miranda. It had taken him a long time to get over the heartbreak when Serena dumped him and he surely didn't want to set himself up for another one. He would just concentrate on his ranch. He still had his buddy, Tramp, who was the son of Hero. He knew Tramp would be very lonely so he knew what he had to do.

The next day he put an ad in several papers in nearby towns requesting to buy an English Shepherd puppy. The following week he got a call from a lady in Rawlins whose dog had four puppies. They would be ready in another week. He set up an appointment with her and was looking forward to getting a new puppy or possibly two. He knew Tramp would be excited.

The following week he went into Rawlins to look at the puppies. He could hardly wait to see them. This is pathetic he thought to himself. I am a grown man and here I am acting like a child. He pulled into the driveway at the address the lady had given him. He got out and went to the door. Before he could ring the doorbell the door swung open. "You must be Eli," said a very attractive middle aged lady. "I'm Jeannie. It's nice to meet you."

"Likewise," replied Eli. "I guess you know I'm here to see the puppies. I have an English Shepherd at home named Tramp and recently had to have his father put down. That's why I am here today; I need to get another playmate for Tramp. He is very lonely."

"I see. Have you considered getting more than one?" she asked.

"I hadn't thought about it but I may change my mind after seeing them."

"Follow me." She led the way to an outside building and opened the door. Inside he could see the Mommy and her babies. They were so cute! "There are three females and one male. You can take your pick."

"I was thinking about getting another male. You know I might take one of each. That way they could grow up together."

"That would be nice. Just pick out the two you want."

So Eli looked for a minute and picked up the female he chose from the three. She was black and white with a white streak running down her nose and some brown on her head. There was no choosing of the males since there was only one. His coloring was similar to that of the female. Eli picked him up and the two were an arm full. They were wiggling so much that he could hardly hold them. He put them back down, paid Jeannie and thanked her. Then he picked them back up and headed for his truck. He put them in the box he had brought to haul one puppy in. They would be crowded but hopefully they would sleep on the ride home. He was lucky that's just what they did. When he arrived home Tramp was there to greet him. He was wondering how Tramp would react to his new brother and sister. It didn't take long to find out. Eli put the puppies on the ground and Tramp got so excited. He was prancing around and sniffing the puppies. Eli was thinking and wishing he could know what was going through Tramp's mind at this moment. One thing for sure he was very excited.

The puppies needed a name. Eli thought for awhile and decided to call them Mack and Molly. That seemed to suit them and would be simple names for the puppies to learn. Jeannie said they'd had their first shots so he would contact Miranda and get them scheduled for their next ones.

Eli called Miranda the next day. Jade answered the phone and he asked to speak to Dr. Sterling.

"May I ask who is calling?" she asked.

"Of course, it's Eli Warren," he replied.

"Just a minute and I'll page her."

"Thank you!"

"Dr. Sterling speaking," said a pleasant voice a minute later.

"Dr. Sterling, this is Eli Warren."

"Oh Eli, how may I help you?"

"I went out and bought two new puppies. They're English Shepherds and only seven weeks old. They've had their first shots and I was wondering if you would be willing to take Mack and Molly on as your patients."

"Mack and Molly, huh? That's cute! Yes I would be happy to take care of your puppies. Bring them for their second shots in four weeks. That should be about right. I'll transfer you back to Jade and she can set up an appointment for you."

"Thanks so much Dr. Sterling."

"You're welcome."

Eli talked to Jade who set up an appointment in four weeks. That would be a long four weeks as he was already looking forward to seeing Miranda again. He was sure she didn't realize what a crush he had on her. "Listen to me," he said aloud. "I sound like a school boy. I need to get over that."

Chapter 12

Meanwhile, things were going well with Miranda and Ethan. She could tell he was falling for her, and she didn't know how to stop him short of breaking up with him. He was wanting more and more of her time. She was having to cancel dates with Morgan and she didn't like that. She was afraid he would stop calling her and she enjoyed his company. She loved the motorcycle rides they went on. She didn't want to give him up. Then there was Eli. He crossed her mind every now and then. Here she was already in two relationships and thinking about a third. "I can't do that," she said aloud.

She threw herself into her work and tried not to think about the men in her life. Karen had warned her, but did she listen? Of course not! Oh, if only Mardi was alive...she wouldn't have this problem. She would be on the ranch back in Montana with him and the rest of her family. Life sure had dealt her a blow. She knew she had to pick up the pieces and move on, and that was what she was trying to do. She was feeling sorry for herself and decided to call her sister Jennifer.

"Hello, Dr. Parker speaking."

"Hi Jennifer, it's your sister."

"Oh, hello Miranda! How are you? This is a surprise! Is everything okay?"

"I'm doing okay I guess. I've got myself into a pickle I think."

"What's going on out there?"

"Well it seems I am dating two guys and thinking about a third one," Miranda sighed.

"Miranda what are you thinking? To date TWO men at one time is trouble enough let alone three."

"I know Jennifer. I didn't think it would get complicated but it has."

"Tell me exactly what's going on!" exclaimed Jennifer.

"Well, I started dating Morgan Cole who owns a Harley Motorcycle Shop in Casper. Of course he rides a Harley and I am having such a good time with him. I love riding and feeling free as the wind. Then along came Ethan Kane who is Sheriff of Carbon County. He is very likeable and I really enjoy his company. Then I met Eli Warren on WESTERN DAY and he is on my mind quite often. There is something about him that I can't quite put my finger on. He seems familiar, but I can't figure it out. He seems very mysterious."

"Little sister, I think you're in a mess. Just what do you plan to do?"

"Truthfully I don't know. That's why I called you. I am hoping you can help me."

"Leave the third one alone and stop thinking about him. To you he is just a stranger and you need to keep it that way. Now for the two you are dating...you need to make a choice. Make a list of pros and cons on both of them. If you write it down that could help you to make a decision."

"I hadn't thought of that. Thanks Sis!"

"I think you'll find life more enjoyable once you settle down to one guy. It will eliminate a lot of stress."

"I know that. Sometimes I get on a tight schedule," laughed Miranda.

"You don't need that in your life Miranda! You need to enjoy your daughter, your job and the company of ONE man!"

"I know you are right, Jennifer, and I promise I will do something about it soon."

"Good! Keep me posted on how things work out."

"I will."

Miranda felt better after she talked to Jennifer. Her big sister always seemed to know the answer. She was so thankful for Jennifer.

The next few weeks went by and she hardly gave Eli a thought. She broke things off with Morgan the next time they went out and he seemed to be somewhat heartbroken. She confessed that she had been seeing another guy and Morgan wanted to know who it was. She reluctantly told him and he seemed to be shocked. She told him she was very sorry and wished him the best. He thanked her and told her he was not looking to settle down anyway and perhaps it was for the best. She agreed with him. She felt like a load was lifted from her shoulders. After Morgan brought her home that night she immediately called her sister and gave her the news. Jennifer was proud of her and told her she did the right thing.

The next morning as she looked at her appointment book she saw that Eli was bringing his puppies for their shots. Oh no... she was thinking...just when I am forgetting him...

At nine o'clock he entered the clinic with his two English Shepherd puppies. Jade looked up as he entered carrying the puppies. "Oh how cute!" she exclaimed. "May I hold one?"

"Of course," Eli replied as he handed her the girl.

"What are their names?"

"Mack and Molly."

"I like that and I think it suits them very well," she said. "Dr. Sterling will be with you shortly."

"Thanks!"

About that time Miranda opened the door and asked him to come in. "How are you doing today and how are the puppies?"

"We're all fine," he answered with a smile.

Miranda examined the puppies then gave them their second shots. They whimpered a little but it never lasted long. They seemed to be happy puppies and were wiggling so much that Eli could hardly hold them. He didn't seem to mind at all since he had a big grin on his face.

"Thanks, Dr. Sterling."

"You're welcome, Eli. Bring them back in a month for their third shot."

"I'll do that," he replied as he left. He stopped to pay and Jade told him she would send him a bill since he had his hands full. He gave her the address and left.

Miranda was very busy the rest of the day and she was glad. That way she didn't have time to let her mind dwell on Eli. She wished she could figure him out but she didn't have a clue as to where to start. *I just need to forget him except for when he brings his dogs to the clinic.*

Meanwhile, Eli let his mind wander all the way home. He pulled into his driveway and actually wondered how he ever made it home. His mind certainly wasn't on his driving because it was on Miranda. He knew she was dating two guys and he wasn't going to interfere. He hadn't heard that she had broken up with Morgan. Would that have set his mind at ease? Probably not, because that could possibly mean that she was getting serious about Ethan. Forget her he told himself.

Three days later when he went to the barn to check on one of his mares who was about to foal, he knew right away there was trouble. He had checked on her the night before and she was fine. Sometime during the night she had gone into labor. She was lying on her side and breathing heavily. She never even seemed to notice when he stooped down beside her. "Now girl," he said. "I can see you need help and I am going to call that beautiful Veterinarian to come help you." The mare looked up at him as if she understood the words he said. He patted her on the head as he took out his cell phone. He was glad he had programmed both of Miranda's numbers into his phone. He called her home phone since it was early.

"Hello," said an unfamiliar voice.

"This is Eli Warren. May I speak to Dr. Sterling? It's an emergency."

"Certainly. Just a moment and I will get her."

"Thanks!"

Miranda picked up the phone. "Hello Eli. How may I help you?"

"I have a mare about ready to foal but there's a problem. She needs more help than I can give her. Can you come to the ranch?"

"Let me get dressed and I'll be there in about twenty minutes."

"Thank you so much!"

Miranda got dressed without showering and headed to the ranch. Eli met her at the house and led the way to the barn. "Thank you so much for coming!" he exclaimed. "It's so good to have you close. I am afraid she might not make it until I could get a vet here from another town."

"I'm more than happy to come to your ranch, Eli. I am doing what I love to do. It doesn't matter what kind of animal it is. I'm just a doctor of animals"

He turned and gave her a smile. "I hope Medicine Bow realizes how blessed they are to have you."

"I think they do," she replied.

They walked into the barn stall where the mare was laying. She was moaning by now. Miranda put on long rubber gloves and proceeded to examine her. "Oh, she is in trouble and would never be able to have her colt without help. It seems that one of the front legs is turned back under the body. I will have to straighten it."

"Thank God that is all," said Eli.

Miranda was able to pull the leg out from under the colt and get both feet headed toward the entrance of the birthing canal. She gently caught the feet and gave a slight pull. The feet emerged and she pulled a little harder. Soon the legs were out and she saw the nose. "We're getting somewhere now," she said.

"Good," said Eli as he wiped the sweat from his face.

With a little more assistance the colt's head was slowly emerging. She got it by the upper legs and pulled again. This time the shoulders came out and then the rest of it followed. "Congratulations Eli, you have a little mare colt!"

"Thank God!" he exclaimed. "Is the mare going to be okay?"

"I think she will be fine."

Miranda hung around a while longer until the mare and her colt were on their feet. "She's beautiful," remarked Miranda looking at the colt.

"Yes she is," said Eli with a huge grin.

"I'll be back to check on them after I close the office this evening."

"Thanks, Miranda!"

She left and went home to take a shower and get ready for work. She was only an hour late. She had contacted Jade and asked her to move around the morning appointments. Jade had everything organized. Miranda realized how fortunate she was to have someone who was so dependable to leave in charge.

Chapter 13

Everything seemed to be going smoothly at work and in Miranda's social life. She and Ethan were becoming closer. She wasn't exactly sure how she felt about him but she could tell he was in love with her. I hope I am doing the right thing, she thought.

She hadn't seen Karen for a couple weeks. Johnathan was occupying most of Karen's free time. Things seemed to be going really well for them. Miranda wouldn't be surprised to hear there was going to be a wedding. She knew Karen was crazy about Johnathan. She was very happy for her Best Friend. She decided to give her a call.

"Hello... Karen speaking."

"Hi Karen, it's Miranda."

"Oh hi Miranda! How are things going?"

"Good. I am staying very busy plus trying to find time for Ethan. Sometimes I think dating is too hard when you have a job and a small child," said Miranda.

"I don't know how you balance it Miranda! I do have it easier since my son Patrick is older and in college. Even though they grow up you never quit worrying about them."

"I'm sure that is true. I am so blessed to have our wonderful nanny Sallie. Without her it really would be hard to cope."

"So how are things going with Ethan?"

"Good, I guess."

"You don't sound very convincing," said Karen. "Do you miss Morgan?"

"To be honest, yes I do! I loved the long motorcycle rides we went on. I guess all good things come to an end sooner or later. I know dating one guy at a time is hard enough and my sister convinced me to make a choice."

"Do you feel less stress now?" asked Karen.

"I guess I do but I find myself thinking about Morgan and Eli."

"Eli? When did this happen?"

"I see him from time to time at the clinic when he brings his dogs; then I went to his ranch to deliver a colt. Somehow I can't get him off my mind. There is something mysterious about that man and I am dying to find out what it is."

"I think you DO have a problem Miranda. I wouldn't want to be in your shoes," she laughed.

"I'm going to change the subject Karen. Do you think you could help me plan a party for Taylor's third birthday? I just want something small for the family and a few friends."

"Sure Miranda, I will be glad to help you. Will your family be coming?"

"I think my sister, Jennifer, and her family will come. My brother, Jordan, and his family may come. The rest of them live too far away."

"Great, I would love to meet your family."

"Do you think the Community Hall would be available in three weeks?"

"I'll have to check the calendar and see. I'm assuming you want Saturday."

"Yes, if it's available. If not, Sunday would work."

Two days later she got a call from Karen telling her that Saturday was available. Miranda was glad and gave Jennifer a call. After talking to her sister she felt a little depressed. It seems that Jennifer and her two daughters would be the only ones coming for the party. Gabe was too busy on the ranch and just couldn't take time off now. Even though she was disappointed Miranda did understand. He did send his love and HAPPY BIRHTDAY wishes to Taylor. Jordan and Hailey were unable to come at this time also. Again Miranda was disappointed, but she knew it was a long drive for them.

Every evening for the next couple of weeks Miranda and Karen worked getting the invitations sent out and decorating the Community Hall. "Miranda, are you inviting Eli?" asked Karen.

"Do you think I should? I have thought about it but didn't know if I should."

"I think you should invite him. After all he is one of your admirers."

"I'm not sure Ethan will be happy about it."

"What difference does it make? Ethan doesn't own you...at least not yet!"

"I know," sighed Miranda. "Go ahead and fix an invitation for Eli."

Karen did just that and smiled as she was writing the invitation. Between the two guys she liked Eli better. She would never tell Miranda because she didn't want to influence her on choosing between the two men. She would just nudge her in the right direction every time she had the chance.

Jennifer, Isabelle, and Rachel Rose arrived in Medicine

Bow on Friday before Taylor's party. It was a happy reunion between the sisters and the cousins. Jennifer was quite impressed with Miranda's clinic and her apartment which looked like something out of a magazine.

"You did a great job with your decorating, Miranda!" exclaimed Jennifer, smiling.

"Thanks! I am pleased the way everything turned out."

They were all up early the next morning. Taylor was too young to understand what was going on but she seemed to be in a very good mood. She loved having her cousins here to play with her. They got dressed and went to the Community Hall about twenty minutes before time to start. People were already gathering in. They had invited about fifty people.

Eli arrived shortly after Miranda. He went straight to her. "Hello Miranda!" he exclaimed. "It's good to see you again. So I finally get to meet your daughter."

"Yes Eli. This is Taylor, who is turning three in a couple of days."

"Nice to meet you, Taylor," he said as he stooped down to her level. He said a few words to her and she hugged him around his neck. Miranda was stunned. Taylor was never like this with a stranger, especially a man.

"Wow Eli, what did you say to her? She is never that friendly with a stranger."

"It was my charm," he teased with a smile. He was still standing there talking to Miranda when Ethan arrived and headed straight toward them.

"Well, well," said Ethan sarcastically. "What do we have here?" Before anyone could say anything he turned to Eli and asked in the same tone. "Just what are you doing here with Miranda?"

Eli spoke in a gentle voice, "I'm only here for Taylor's birthday party. That's all."

"As far as I'm concerned you have no right to be here!"

"Now Ethan...Eli was invited so he must be treated like the other guests. I would appreciate it if this conversation would come to an end immediately!" exclaimed Miranda.

Ethan walked away without even answering Miranda. At that moment Miranda didn't care. He was out of place, and besides, he doesn't own me she thought.

"Miranda I am SO sorry for causing you trouble!" exclaimed Eli. "I never intended for anything like this to happen."

"I know you didn't Eli, and it's okay!"

"I guess I shouldn't have come."

"I am glad you did," she said as she placed her hand on his hard, muscled upper arm.

"Perhaps I should go."

"NO! I want you to stay," said Miranda. "I apologize for the way Ethan acted."

"That's okay. I might do the same if you were my girl," he replied with a laugh.

"I couldn't see you acting like that!"

"Actually, I wouldn't. I would never try to hold on to anything that wasn't really mine."

"I like your way of thinking, Eli."

"Thanks. Perhaps I had better mingle and let Ethan come back to you."

"Okay, and thanks for coming!" She was wishing he would stay there with her.

"Thanks for the invitation. I wouldn't have missed coming for anything in the world!"

She watched him walk away and her heart dropped.

Why was she feeling this way when she was supposed to be in love with Ethan? Things were surely in a mess! What was she going to do? When she went for a period of time without seeing Eli she could do pretty well. Then when she caught a glimpse of him it all came flooding back. This mysterious man had a hold on her and she didn't have a clue what it was. What was she going to do? Please, Dear God...tell me what to do.

Chapter 14

Taylor's party was over and Jennifer, Isabelle, and Rachel Rose went back home to Montana. Miranda was sad to see them leave, but they promised to come back again soon.

Ethan had left the party early and hadn't called Miranda for a few days. She was determined not to call him either. Let him sulk, she thought. He is a grown man and he should know better. No one had ever 'owned' her, and she wasn't going to allow it now.

Finally he called her five days later. "How are you Miranda?" he asked.

"I am just fine," she answered in a nonchalant manner.

"Have you been busy?"

"Of course I have. I am always busy."

"Have you seen Eli?"

"Not since the party. Why?"

"Oh I just figured he would ask you out."

"For your information he didn't!" she exclaimed.

"Now don't get defensive."

"Actually, it's none of your business if Eli did ask me out!"

"REALLY?"

"Yes really! I don't belong to you or any other man!"

"I'm sorry to hear that. I was about to ask you to marry me."

"YOU WHAT?"

"Will you marry me, Miranda?" he asked.

"This is too sudden. I will have to be in a better mood when I give you an answer. Besides I don't like being proposed to over the phone!"

"I'm sorry, Miranda. This was NOT the way I planned it."

"We need to forget this subject for now."

"As you wish, my dear."

Time passed by and they dated once a week. Ethan called her almost every night during the week. Sometimes she actually didn't have time to talk but didn't want to tell him for fear of sounding rude. Other than that things were going really well between them. He told her over and over how much he loved her. She loved him too, but it was not the kind of love she had felt for Mardi. He was the love of her life and she never expected to feel that way about anyone else. Not ever!

Finally one night about three months later while they were at a nice restaurant eating, he suddenly knelt down on one knee and pulled a box out of his pocket. He opened the box and put it on the table. "Dr. Miranda Sterling...will you marry me?"

Miranda sat there with her mouth open. "Ethan I am surprised!" she exclaimed. "I don't know what to say!"

"Say 'YES'!"

"Yes, I will marry you Ethan."

He could tell she didn't sound too enthused but she would learn to love him as much as he loved her. It might take some time but she would one day. He would be patient with her.

He placed the large diamond engagement ring on her finger. She smiled as best she could. She didn't want him to think she was ungrateful but something just didn't feel right. Maybe time would take care of that. At least she hoped it would. Ethan was a fine man and any girl would be lucky to have him. She kept telling herself how lucky she was.

After he took her home her first call was to Karen. "Karen, guess what?" She didn't wait for Karen to guess. "I'm engaged! Ethan gave me a beautiful diamond tonight at dinner."

"Congratulations, Miranda! I am so happy for you. By the way, you are getting a good man!"

"I know...I am a lucky woman!"

"Indeed you are! When's the wedding?" asked an anxious Karen.

"Oh we haven't set a date yet. I don't want to rush into anything."

"Smart girl!"

"I just wanted to let you know. In fact I called you first. Now I need to call my sister. Have a good night and we'll talk later Karen."

Miranda called her sister next. Jennifer was very happy to hear the news. "I hope you're getting a good man. I must say I didn't like what he did at Taylor's birthday party."

"That hasn't happened anymore. He is a perfect gentleman!"

"Let's just hope he stays that way AFTER you marry him!"

"I think he will."

Miranda also called her brothers, Rob, Jordan and Blake. They all congratulated her and assured her they would be there for the wedding. She told them she would let them know as soon as a date was set. Before she finished talking to the last one of her brothers she had a beep. She saw it was Ethan and she never took the call. She knew she could return his call. Ten minutes later she dialed his number. "Hello Ethan," she said.

"Hi Miranda. Why didn't you answer the phone when I called?"

"I was talking with my brothers."

"As long as it was your brothers then it's okay!"

"What does that mean? Are you screening my calls?" she asked angrily.

"NO, NO, NO! That's not what I meant!"

"Just what did you mean?"

"I guess I just don't want you talking to other men."

"I'm sorry Ethan...I have to talk to other men. My business requires it and I will not be told who I can or cannot talk to. Do you understand that?"

"I'm sorry," he replied without saying yes he understood.

"I have to go to bed now. I have an early day tomorrow. Goodnight Ethan."

She hung up the phone, pulled off the ring and went to bed. She lay there thinking and thinking. Sleep did not come for a long time. She lay there wondering if she was doing the right thing. She prayed and asked God to supply her with the husband he had prepared for her. She felt relief and drifted off to sleep.

Ethan called her early the next morning and things seemed as normal as ever. Neither of them mentioned the conversation of the night before. He was in a good mood and told her how much he loved her. She was not prepared for what came out of his mouth next. "Let's get married in a couple months."

"WHAT? You're kidding, right?"

"No, I am serious. What's the use in waiting?" he asked.

"I think we should be sure we are doing the right thing."

"I'm certain...I just hope you are!"

"I know...let's have an engagement party."

He hesitated before speaking and then asked, "Why would you want to do that?"

"I think it would be nice to share our happy news with the town people."

"As long as that old cowboy doesn't come!" exclaimed Ethan with a frown.

"What do you have against Eli? He hasn't done anything to you! For your information he will be invited! He is one of my customers at the clinic."

"Does that mean you're inviting ALL of them?"

"That's exactly what it means and you can get over it or there'll be no wedding!" Miranda was feeling unnerved by now and she intended to set Ethan straight once and for all.

"Oh no Miranda...please don't say that. I'll try to do better," he promised.

By now she was beginning to wonder. True to his word he was the perfect gentleman for the next several months. So Miranda decided to go ahead and plan their engagement party. With the help of her friend, Karen, things went very smoothly. Miranda seemed to be very happy and it showed to anyone who was around her. All her family had been invited but only Jennifer was coming. That seemed to be the story of her life. She was beginning to wonder if moving away from the ranch was a good thing. Surely they would all come for the wedding.

Chapter 15

Meanwhile out on the ranch things were difficult for Eli. He had just received Miranda's Engagement Party invitation. This put him in a depressed mood. He knew he had no right to feel this way. After all she was not his and never had been. He would just continue to worship her from afar. He decided to invite her to the ranch where he could have a talk with her. So he gave her a call that night. She was coming over the next evening after work. He decided to cook dinner for her in hopes she wouldn't eat before coming. He wanted to surprise her.

Shortly after five o'clock Miranda pulled into his driveway. She wondered what he wanted to discuss with her. She never told Ethan she was going to the ranch.

Eli met her at the door with a big smile on his face. "Welcome, Miranda! Glad you could come over. Come on in. Dinner is almost ready."

"Dinner? Now that is a nice surprise. I am starving."

"I thought you might be," he added with a chuckle.

"Thank you! This is so sweet of you!"

They had a wonderful dinner with lots of great conversation. Miranda felt so at ease with Eli. There was just something about him that captivated her. It was like she had always known him and she knew that wasn't true. She wished she could figure him out.

After they finished eating Eli spoke up, "There is someone I want to introduce you to." He got up and left the room and returned with a small dark haired girl. "This is my daughter Savannah. She is eight years old."

Miranda was stunned. He had never mentioned a daughter. "Hello Savannah," replied Miranda. "Nice to meet you!"

"Hello," said a shy Savannah.

"What a beautiful little girl you are. You look just like your daddy."

"Thanks," replied Eli. "Savannah you can go back to your room now."

The little girl left without saying another word. Miranda's heart went out to this little girl. She turned to Eli and asked, "Why didn't you tell me about Savannah before now? I can't believe that no one said a word about her."

"I did ask Karen not to tell you. I wanted to introduce you to her. She is a lonely little girl. I was wondering if we might take our girls to the park one day. It would be good for Savannah to be with another child even if she is younger."

"I think we could arrange that."

"Thank you so much Miranda! It will mean a lot to Savannah and me."

"I guess I'm just curious but where is her mother?"

"She died a couple weeks after Savannah was born."

"I am so sorry. I had no idea."

"It was a very hard time for me with losing Susan and having a baby to raise on my own. I had to hire a full time housekeeper. Donna has been a real blessing to our family.

She's a good Christian lady and has taught Savannah good morals and told her about Jesus."

"That's wonderful!"

He seemed to have said all he wanted to on the subject and turned to Miranda and asked, "Would you like to take a walk?"

"Sure, that would be nice."

So they left the house and walked for an hour. They went by the stable where Miranda looked in on the new mare colt that had grown quite a lot. When Miranda turned to walk out of the stable, Eli put his arms around her and pulled her to him. Without saying a word he leaned over and passionately kissed her. Her heart was fluttering as she returned his kiss. Then it was over...

"I am so sorry!" he exclaimed. "I had no right to do that."

"It's okay Eli. It was my fault too. We must keep this between us. You know I'm going to marry Ethan."

"I know...and again I am so sorry."

They walked out of the stable and headed for the house. Miranda's heart was still beating fast. She was wondering how she let this happen. There was nothing she could have done to prevent it. In fact she rather enjoyed it. He was an excellent kisser. She caught herself comparing him to Ethan. I have to get over this she told herself. Soon I will be marrying another man. This man Eli Warren had left his mark on her and she wondered if she would ever be FREE of him. At this moment she wasn't sure she wanted to be free of him. I sure have gotten myself in a mess she thought.

As they arrived back at the beautiful log house Miranda told Eli she must go. He looked her straight in the eye and told her he'd had a wonderful evening.

"Me too!" she exclaimed. "Call me when you have time and we'll set up a play date for the girls."

"Sounds good to me," he said with a big grin.

Miranda got into her car and left. She tried not to let Eli see how shaken she actually was. He was on her mind all the way home. She had never in her life been kissed the way he kissed her. She would never forget this day even if she lived to be one hundred years old.

As soon as she walked in the door Sallie informed her that Ethan had called three times. "He wanted to know where you were and I told him you were seeing a client," said Sallie with a smile.

"Good for you Sallie. You're learning!"

Several minutes later the phone rang again. This time Miranda answered after seeing it was Ethan. "Hello Ethan."

"Where have you been?" he asked. She could hear the agitation in his voice.

"I had to call on a client."

"Male or female?"

"What difference does it make? They're all the same to me. Drop the subject and tell me why you really called," she said.

"No reason in particular. I just wanted to talk to you."

"Okay...talk!"

"I love you, Miranda."

"I know you do Ethan." For some reason she could not tell him she loved him. Right at this moment she wasn't sure how she felt about him. He really gets under her skin by not trusting her. Jealously is one thing she couldn't stand. They talked for a few more minutes and she told him she had to go.

Three days later she received a call from Eli. Again he

apologized for his behavior. He told her he would be free on Friday and asked how her schedule was. "Would that be a good day to take the girls to the park?"

"I think I can arrange it. Meet me there at eleven o'clock. I will bring a picnic basket and we'll have lunch together."

"That sounds wonderful! I know Savannah will like that!"

"Great. Then it's settled. I will see you Friday morning at eleven o'clock."

"I'll be looking forward to it," he replied.

"Me too!"

When she got off the phone she dialed Karen. She wanted to get her opinion on this outing. After telling Karen her plans she asked her opinion.

"Well my dear Miranda I think you are doing the right thing. This will be good therapy for Savannah. She doesn't get out much and has some issues of dealing with people. So just put this down as a human 'doctor' call."

"I hadn't thought of it like that."

Miranda was glad when Friday came. She got Taylor and herself ready for their day in the park with Eli and Savannah. The picnic basket was packed and ready to go. Sallie had fixed the food for them. She was so grateful to have her in their home. She was a part of their family. Miranda was really looking forward to spending time with Eli and his daughter. She hadn't mentioned it to Ethan. After all it would only upset him and she was doing nothing wrong. She was helping a friend with his child.

Eli and Savannah were already there when Miranda pulled into the parking lot. They all got out of their cars and walked toward each other. Miranda noticed what a pleasant smile Eli had. He was very good looking and smiling enhanced his looks. Savannah was not smiling but looked rather sad. Miranda's heart went out to her. "Hello Eli...Hi Savannah. How are you doing today? Are you ready to eat and play?"

Eli responded with, "We're fine and yes we are looking forward to our day in the park."

"Good," said Miranda. "Sallie packed our lunch so I have no idea what we are having."

"Surprises are most always good." He looked at Miranda and smiled.

"Savannah, I would like for you to meet my daughter, Taylor."

"Hi Taylor," said Savannah softly.

Taylor looked at her and asked," Did you come to play with me?"

Savannah looked at her dad then back at Taylor and replied, "I guess."

Miranda picked a table and spread the tablecloth over it. She opened the basket and the smell of Fried Chicken was awesome. Sallie was a wonderful cook. There was potato salad, slaw, baked beans and fresh homemade rolls along with apple pie and brownies.

"This looks wonderful!" exclaimed Eli. "Please thank Sallie for all this wonderful food and thank you Miranda for sharing this day with us."

"You are most welcome Eli. I am happy to be here with you and Savannah."

After they finished eating, the girls went to play on the swings. There was a small one with a slide for Taylor. Savannah was taking care of her like a little mom. Eli smiled as he watched her. Miranda could tell he was proud of his daughter. This was becoming a very special day to Miranda. She wished she knew what Eli was thinking. She sure was enjoying his company. She had slipped off her engagement ring before leaving home this morning.

Somehow it didn't seem right to be wearing it while she was in the company of Eli. She wondered if he noticed. If he did he never mentioned it to her.

Later in the afternoon they said goodbye and each went their separate way. It had been a wonderful time for all of them. Savannah was actually smiling when they left. She and Taylor had so much fun.

As Miranda and Taylor were driving home she asked, "Will I see Vanna again?"

"Oh sweetie I don't know. You had a good time with Savannah didn't you?"

"Uh huh," she said. "I like Vanna."

"Maybe we can get together another day. I might even take you out to the ranch where they live. Would you like that?"

"Yeah," she answered so excited. "When can we go Mommy?"

"Maybe one day soon."

Eli and Savannah had a longer drive so that meant more time for conversation. "Did you have a good time today Savannah?"

"Yes Daddy. Taylor was fun. I like playing with her. She seems older than three."

"She is around adults all the time so I guess that's why she acts so grown up."

"Can we see them again?" she asked smiling at her dad.

"I hope so Savannah. I really hope so. I was thinking that maybe we could invite them to the ranch to spend the day."

"Oh, Daddy, I would love that. I could show Taylor my horse and maybe we could ride."

"You can show her your horse but she is too little to

ride unless her mother would take her for a ride. We'll have to wait and see."

"Oh, Daddy, I am so excited!"

"That's great, Kitten! I'm so glad to see you happy!"

Chapter 16

Things continued as normal with Miranda and Ethan. He saw her every Saturday and called her about every day. One day at the beginning of their conversation he spoke frankly, "Miranda, I think it's time to set the date for the Engagement Party. I think one month would give you time to get everything ready."

"It would rush me but I think I can do it with Karen's help."

"Good!" he exclaimed. "I'm tired of waiting!"

"Four weeks from this Saturday it will be. I will be very busy so I won't be able to talk on the phone every night."

"I understand. I will try to refrain from calling."

"Good, as I need as much time as I can get if I am going to pull this thing off."

"This thing?" he asked.

"Oh Ethan you know what I mean! I need to call Karen. Do you mind if we get off the phone now?"

"Okay," he said sounding disgruntled.

Miranda called Karen immediately and told her the

plans. "Sure I will help you get it all together, Miranda. That's what friends are for!"

"Thank you Karen! I don't know what I would do without you!"

"I just have one question for you Miranda. Are you sure you are doing the right thing?"

"I hope so," answered Miranda.

"What kind of an answer is that?"

Miranda laughed and said, "Yes, Karen I do love Ethan."

"What about Eli?"

"He is a good friend."

"You know I love you like a sister Miranda. I just don't want you to make a mistake!"

"Thanks for caring so much Karen!"

Two weeks went by and the invitations were ready to be mailed. Miranda was getting excited and YES she did send one to Eli. Two days after receiving the invitation Eli gave her a call. He told himself he would NOT mention the invitation to her.

"Hello Miranda. How are you doing?" he asked.

"I'm fine, but very busy." She didn't mention what was keeping her so busy.

"You need to take some time and relax Miranda. I just had a thought...why don't you and Taylor come to the ranch and spend the day this Saturday?"

"Saturday is my date night."

"Come early and that way you can leave in time to get home for your date."

"Are you twisting my arm?" she laughed.

"Is that what you think?" he asked with a laugh.

"Okay, we will do it. That sounds like a relaxing day and Lord knows I need that."

"It's a date then...we'll be looking for you on Saturday around eleven o'clock. Savannah will be so happy!"

"So will Taylor. We'll be there."

Miranda immediately called Karen and told her the plans. "Am I doing the right thing?' she asked.

"Frankly, I think you are."

"I think I have to tell Eli this will be the last time I can see him. I feel guilty seeing him behind Ethan's back even though Eli and I are only friends. Our daughters love playing together also."

"I was going to call you later today. I have some GREAT news! Johnathan has asked me to marry him!!!"

"CONGRATULATIONS!!! Johnathan is one lucky man!!! So have you set a date yet?"

"No, we haven't discussed every detail yet. He did tell me that he doesn't want to risk losing me to another man."

"Now that sounds like a smart man!" exclaimed Miranda.

Karen laughed and replied, "I am so happy that he has chosen me for his wife. We have so much in common and love being together."

"I am so happy for you Karen!"

"Thanks, Miranda! Will you be my Maid of Honor or Matron of Honor whichever your status is at the time?"

"Of course, Karen. I would be honored! You also know that I am planning on you being in my wedding too."

"I would be honored to walk down the aisle for you."

Miranda woke up Saturday morning to a beautiful day. The sun was shining in through the blinds and she could hear birds singing. "Thank you God for such a glorious day," she prayed aloud. "Help me today and give me the words I need to say to Eli. Please help him to understand. In Jesus name I pray, AMEN."

They left the house and arrived at the ranch shortly before eleven o'clock. Savannah was sitting on the front porch waiting for them. She got up and came to meet them with a big smile on her face. "Hello Savannah," said Miranda. "How are you today?"

"Good," Savannah replied with a smile. She walked over and took Taylor's hand. "Do you want to go play?"

"Yes," said Taylor. Savannah took her hand and off they went to her playhouse in the yard. It was such a cute little log cottage which resembled the main house. There was a log swing set and slide beside it. How nice of Eli to build this for Savannah. It was such a wonderful place for her to play. She seemed so excited to have Taylor to play with.

After Miranda greeted Eli she asked if she could see Savannah's playhouse. They walked over and went inside where the girls were already playing with dolls. This was exactly what Taylor loved. Miranda was glad she had brought her over to play with Savannah. Seeing how much fun she was having made Miranda wonder how in the world she could deny Taylor this pleasure. She could also see how much it was helping Savannah. She didn't have that sad look on her face anymore. Taylor seemed to be good therapy for her.

Miranda and Eli turned and walked out the door and headed to the main house where Donna was busy packing a picnic basket for them.

"Smells good, Donna!" exclaimed Eli.

"It surely does," agreed Miranda. "We appreciate you fixing our food."

"Oh you're welcome," said Donna smiling. "It's part of my job."

She handed the basket to Eli and they went to get the girls who were so busy playing, that they actually didn't want to stop long enough to eat. With a little persuasion they followed their parents to a big Oak tree and sat down at the picnic table.

Miranda spread the tablecloth over the table then she and Eli began to unpack the basket. Donna had outdone herself. There was a little bit of everything to eat. Suddenly Miranda felt very hungry. It was always good to eat someone else's cooking.

They sat down to eat and Eli said the blessing. Miranda could feel so much reverence in his prayer. She knew he was a good Christian man. Some woman would be very lucky to have him for a husband. If only it wasn't for Ethan...

She helped Eli clean up when they finished eating. The girls went back to the playhouse while Eli and Miranda settled on the front porch. They decided to sit in the swing. Miranda had grown up with a swing and dearly loved it. She felt so comfortable sitting beside Eli. How can I tell him? She decided now was not the time. They engaged in a lively conversation and talked about many things. She was getting to know him better all the time and she really liked what she knew about him.

A frown crossed Eli's face as he brought up the subject, "It's only two weeks until your Engagement Party right?"

"Yes, that's correct."

"Are you excited?"

She hesitated a few seconds and replied, "I guess."

"That doesn't sound too convincing!"

"I have a lot on my mind," she said with a sigh.

"Well let's forget all that today and enjoy being together as this will probably be our last time."

"She looked up at him with tears in her eyes and spoke, "I can't think about that!"

She saw a tear roll down his face and drop onto his

shirt. She wanted to reach out and give him a hug but she refrained. She stood up and told him it was time for them to go. She had to get away from him...

Chapter 17

Ethan picked her up at seven o'clock that night. He seemed to be in a good mood but he noticed that she seemed to be far away in her thoughts as they were driving to the restaurant. "A penny for your thoughts," he teased.

"Sorry Ethan. I guess I've just got a lot on my mind. With the Engagement Party getting so close I am wondering if we'll have everything done in time."

"Is there anything I can do to help?"

"Just give me more time at night to work on things. I love for you to call but right now I am really pushed for time."

"Okay Miranda. I will try to call less or at least not talk as long."

"I think that would help."

They rode around a while after dinner. Miranda developed a headache and asked Ethan to take her home. She apologized for calling the evening short but she just had to get home. She needed to lie down and rest. He said he understood and left as soon as he dropped her off at her house.

Sallie met her at the door. "You're home early. Is something wrong?"

"I have a terrible headache."

"I'm sorry. Is there anything I can do?"

"I don't think so. I am going to take a couple of Tylenol pills and lie down."

"Taylor is already in bed, so don't worry about her."

"Thank you so much Sallie. I couldn't make it without you."

The next two weeks passed quickly and Miranda was very busy. Karen helped her as much as she possibly could. Finally the big day came. Miranda spent the day pondering over her life since she had been in Medicine Bow. She hoped she was doing the right thing in marrying Ethan. Her mind told her she was but her heart didn't quite agree with her mind.

The party was at four o'clock and that was only two hours away. Miranda and Karen had agreed to meet at the Community Hall at two o'clock. She got herself dressed and looked in the mirror. "I'm not seeing happiness," she told herself. "What's wrong with me?" She tried to smile but that didn't come easy. She knew she had to put on a HAPPY FACE.

That was the first thing Karen noticed about her when they met. "Girl, are you sure you're doing the right thing?"

"I just don't know Karen! I'm in too deep now to call it off. I guess I'll just go ahead with the plans."

"At least this is NOT the wedding. Thank goodness you will have time to think this out before then."

Miranda gave her a hug and thanked her for being such a good friend. Karen smiled and said she would always be there for her. She could see all the happiness in Karen's face and she was glad. Karen was sure that

Johnathan was the right man for her. They were working on their own wedding plans. Miranda wished her life was as uncomplicated as Karen's was.

The caterer was already there and was setting up the food tables. The food looked delicious and Miranda realized she was actually hungry. She hadn't eaten anything all day. She'd had too much on her mind to be thinking about food.

Ethan arrived around three-thirty. He seemed to be in a good mood and came straight to Miranda and gave her a kiss. He was dressed to the nines and Miranda had to admit he was a very good looking man.

Ten minutes later Eli walked through the front door. Miranda took one look at him and let out a gasp. He was dressed in a black suit, cowboy hat and wearing dark glasses which he removed as he headed toward her. An image from a couple years ago flooded her mind. At that moment she knew she had seen him before she came to Medicine Bow. She remembered that fateful day when Mardi had been laid to rest in the Parker Family Cemetery. She remembered the man in the shadows that only she and Jennifer saw. She knew in her heart that man had been Eli Warren. As he approached her she knew she had to tell him that she remembered him.

"Hello Miranda and Ethan. Congratulations on your engagement!" Eli exclaimed. "I wish you both the best. Take care of her Ethan. She is a very special lady!"

"Thanks," replied Ethan. "I know Miranda is a special lady and I plan to take care of her and keep her away from men like you!"

"Ethan!" exclaimed Miranda. "I think you should apologize to Eli. That remark was uncalled for!"

"Sorry, man. I just want everyone to know Miranda is MY woman!" Miranda could tell that Ethan resented the attention she received from Eli. That made her halfway mad. If he thought she would never speak to Eli again, he had another thought coming. Eli was her friend and his daughter Savannah was friends with little Taylor. She was not going to take the friendship away from the girls.

The crowd was gathering while music was playing softly in the background. What should have been a happy occasion for Miranda had turned into something more like a funeral. If only Ethan could contain himself and his jealousy. Miranda was wondering if she could deal with this on a daily basis. He seemed to be a very jealous man and that would not make a happy marriage.

People gathered around the buffet tables and filled their plates with an assortment of food. They seemed to enjoy the meal very much. Miranda hardly ate anything. She was so hungry when she arrived but Ethan had diminished her appetite. When everyone finished Ethan's friend Ray stood up and made a toast. "To my good friend Ethan and his beautiful fiancée Miranda, I want to wish you the best in your upcoming marriage and may you have a long happy life together. I've known Ethan since we were young boys. We got into trouble quite often but it was only pranks we used to pull on people. Seriously Ethan is a good guy and you are getting a wonderful man Miranda."

The crowd applauded as Ray sat down. Ethan looked at Miranda who was sitting next to him with no expression on her face. "What's the matter?" he asked.

"Nothing," she replied.

A hush fell over the crowd as Eli Warren rose to his feet and began to speak. "I know this is supposed to be a joyous occasion for Miranda and Ethan but there is something I just have to say. For several months now I have been around Miranda and shared time with her. I don't know if Ethan knows or not. I never asked and she never told. As we gather here today I just have to speak about my feelings for Miranda."

Everyone was quiet as a mouse and some sat there with gaping mouths. They couldn't believe what they were hearing. Eli was quiet most of the time and they were astonished that he was speaking so frankly.

He continued, "To make a long story short...I have fallen deeply in love with Miranda. I guess you are wondering if I have told her. No, I haven't! I knew she was getting engaged and thought I could keep my feelings about her to myself. I find that is not true. I have to speak now... before it's too late. I can't let her get married without knowing how I feel about her. I don't want her to ever have any regrets."

He sat back down and it was so quiet in the room that you could have heard a pin drop. Then Ethan rose to his feet and headed over to the table where Eli was sitting. "STAND UP!" he said loudly to Eli who rose to his feet. "HOW DARE YOU COME HERE AND EXPRESS YOUR LOVE FOR MIRANDA!!! SHE IS GOING TO MARRY ME AND YOU NEED TO BUTT OUT! I THINK YOU NEED TO LEAVE THIS ROOM IMMEDIATELY."

"Ethan you're acting like a jerk. I hope Miranda will see through you before it's too late."

That set Ethan off. He drew back his fist and hit Eli directly in the face. He never stopped with one blow but administered several blows knocking Eli to the floor. Eli did not fight back but was trying to block Ethan's blows. Miranda jumped up from the table and ran to them. "STOP IT ETHAN!!!" she screamed. She grabbed his coat and pulled as hard as she could. "I AM ASHAMED OF YOU ETHAN!!!"

"Sorry Miranda but Eli had this coming. He's been

after you for several months. Tell me girl, how long have you been involved with Eli? He said you had been spending time together. I want to know EVERYTHING!!!"

"There's nothing to tell. Eli and I are only friends."

"I don't believe that for one minute!"

"At this point I don't care what you believe. I think we should call off the engagement. I don't think a marriage between us would ever work."

"What are you saying? Do you mean you want to break up?"

"That's exactly what I'm saying Ethan!" She pulled off her engagement ring and handed it to him.

"Oh no...That would be too easy for Eli to slip into my place!" he exclaimed as he reluctantly took the ring.

"Ethan I am telling you... you no longer have a place in my life." Miranda turned and faced the crowd, "I am sooo sorry for this outbreak today. I thank each one of you for coming but I must tell you that my engagement to Ethan is over. There will be NO wedding! Go ahead and mingle and try to salvage the rest of the party. I will be leaving immediately. Again I am sorry!" With that she walked back to her table and picked up Taylor. Sallie, Jennifer and her family followed her out the door.

Eli was waiting outside near her car. As she approached he said, "Miranda I am so sorry! I didn't mean to cause you trouble but I had to let you know what was on my heart. I guess I should have told you before today but I could never find the right time. Please accept my apology."

"It's okay Eli. It's not your fault. I should have seen through him before now. I think I did know but kept thinking he would change once we were married. I am glad you opened my eyes to the real truth."

Eli walked to his truck and Miranda got into her car

and drove home. She felt so humiliated. How could she have been so blind?

She was happy to have her sister here with her. She felt bad that they had driven this far to a party that turned into a farce. "Don't worry about us. I am sorry all this happened to you Miranda. You don't deserve it! I'm just glad you found it all out before you married Ethan."

"I know. Thank you for being here for me!"

They talked into the wee hours of the morning. Everyone else was in bed and they felt at ease to share with each other. They had so much catching up to do. Finally at 2:00 a.m. they went to bed. Miranda felt exhausted but sleep did not come easily. She lay there thinking over the events of the previous day and wondered how she could have been so blind. All the signs were there but she looked beyond them and thought things would change. Rarely do things ever change for the better. Finally she went to sleep only to have a bad dream. All the things of yesterday came rushing back and it seemed so real to her. She was reliving it over. She woke up in a cold sweat. When she realized it was only a dream she felt somewhat better. She knew she did the right thing. She lay there and turned her thoughts to Eli. He was a wonderful man. He had confessed his love for her in front of all those people. It took a brave man to do that. Deep in her heart she knew she loved him too. She just had never admitted it. She wondered when and if he would call her. She could call him but she decided it would be best to let him do the calling. She didn't want to appear over anxious.

Jennifer, Gabe and the girls left later that day. They needed to get back to work on Monday. Miranda was sad to see them go but Jennifer promised her they would come back soon. Somehow that relieved her sadness. They said their tearful goodbyes and the Colter family was on their way back home to Montana.

Miranda decided to take a couple days off and try to regain her composure. After lunch on Monday her phone rang. She saw that it was Eli. "Hello Eli," she beamed.

"How are you doing Miranda?" he asked in a pleasant voice. "I've been thinking about you."

"I am doing okay. I'm taking a couple days off work."

"That's what Jade told me. I think you're doing the right thing and again, I am so sorry for all the trouble I caused."

"Don't worry about it Eli. You saved me from making a huge mistake!"

"Really?"

"YES!"

They talked for half an hour. Eli could tell from the tone of her voice that she was feeling better. He was glad he could cheer her up. Then he had an idea... "Miranda since you're not working tomorrow, why don't you and Taylor come out to the ranch and spend the day? Savannah would love it!"

Miranda was quiet for a few seconds and then she said, "I guess we could do that. I know Taylor would be very happy. She loves playing with Savannah."

"Then it's a date!" Eli exclaimed. Miranda could hear the joy in his voice. She was glad but she knew they had to take their time and see where this led them. She still had something she needed to ask him. Maybe tomorrow would be a good time.

She lay awake for quite some time just thinking about the events of yesterday and today. She felt like a big burden had been lifted from her shoulders and this told her she did the right thing. She finally drifted off to sleep and never woke until the sun was shining in the window the next morning. She felt so refreshed and ready for the day. She had a good feeling about a possible relationship with Eli. Time would tell. She got up and went downstairs only to find Sallie and Taylor eating breakfast. She fixed some toast and poured herself a cup of coffee. She was not much on eating breakfast.

"What are your plans for today?" asked Sallie.

"Eli invited us out to the ranch for the day."

"That's nice," Sallie said smiling.

"Taylor and Savannah have such a good time together."

"That's great. I wish all of you the best!"

"Thanks Sallie, but I intend to take it slow this time."

"Smart girl!"

Miranda and Taylor left the house around eleven o'clock and headed to the ranch. Eli and Savannah met them on the porch. Eli gave her a hug then stooped down and hugged Taylor. She put her little arms around his neck and squeezed.

"That's a good hug Taylor!" exclaimed Eli.

Miranda gave Savannah a hug too. She was all smiles and was so happy that they had company.

"Daddy, may we ride the horse?" she asked.

"Yes, you may ride, but Miranda will have to ride with Taylor since she is too small to go by herself."

"Can we go now Daddy...please?"

"Miranda would you like to go for a short ride?" asked Eli.

"Sure! It will be fun," she replied.

So they headed to the stable and Eli picked out a mare named Lily for her to ride. He saddled it and helped her on. Then he lifted Taylor up in front of Miranda. He then saddled Savannah's horse Toby and helped her mount. He then saddled his own horse, Sam, mounted him and off they went. They rode for about an hour then headed back home. Taylor was so excited and loved the ride. They rode into the stable where one of the cowboys was waiting to take care of the horses.

They were all starving by now. Donna had a wonderful lunch prepared for them which they ate on the back patio. Miranda had never felt more at peace than she did right then. I could get used to this, she told herself.

The girls went to the playhouse and left Eli and Miranda alone. She was thinking...I have to ask him. "Eli there is something that's been on my mind for quite a long while and I need to talk to you about it."

"Sure go ahead Miranda."

"You told me you have been to Laurel, Montana."

"That's right. It was a couple years ago."

"My husband, Mardi, was killed a couple of years ago. When Jennifer and I were leaving the Parker Cemetery, we saw a man dressed in a black suit, black cowboy hat and dark glasses. He was only there for a moment then turned and disappeared into the shadows. For some reason I have a feeling it was you. From the first time I met you I felt that I had seen you before. Am I crazy or what? I have to know. Was it you?"

"Yes, it was me," he answered. "I never thought you would ever put two and two together on that. I would have eventually told you."

"What I'm wondering... is why you were there."

"I had been told that the Parker Ranch in Laurel, Montana had a prize bull for sale and that was why I came there. I had no idea I would be interrupting a funeral. I felt so bad and that is why I disappeared as suddenly as possible. When I found no one at the house I ventured farther. That's when I saw the people gathered at the cemetery. I am so sorry Miranda!"

"How could you have known?" she asked.

"If I had known I would never had shown my face there that day!"

"I guess you could call it fate. Isn't it funny how things turn out sometimes? Never in a million years would I have dreamed I would be talking to you today. God works in mysterious ways!"

"He surely does!"

Chapter 18

Miranda and Taylor left later and headed for home. Sallie met them at the door smiling from ear to ear. "What is going on?" asked Miranda. "I have never seen you this happy before!"

"I had a call from my sisters, Emily, and Ethel in Montana. They had some exciting news to tell me. It seems that they had an unexpected call from Bobby. He had tried to call me but found out that my number had been disconnected. Of course he called them to see what was going on. When they told him I had moved to Medicine Bow, Wyoming he was stunned. He never thought I would ever leave home. I guess I showed him didn't I?"

"Wow, Sallie, this is a lot to digest. So what did he want?"

"He told them he needed to talk to me so they gave him this number. He never said when he would call. I guess I am as surprised as you are about this turn of events."

"Please don't read more into this than it is Sallie. He hurt you very badly but don't let him do it again. You don't deserve it. You will be better off if he never contacts you again!"

"I know he has caused me a lot of heartache but I still love him, Miranda. I know I always will! My head tells me to forget him but my heart tells me I never will."

Miranda went over and put her arms around Sallie. "At least you know Taylor and I love you and you will always have a home with us."

"Thank you, Miranda! I don't know what I would do without you!"

"Well, don't even think about it. We'll take care of you."

The next few weeks went by and Miranda could tell Sallie was anxious every time the phone rang. Bobby did not call. Miranda could see the disappointment every time that it wasn't him. It would have been better if her sisters had not told her. She could also understand that they wanted to warn her so she would be prepared if he did call.

Three weeks later the call Sallie longed for came. She was almost in shock when he called. "Hello Sallie," he said.

"Hello," she answered in a soft tone.

"How are things going? I was surprised to hear that you moved from your home in Montana to a faraway place like Medicine Bow."

"I came to help out my good friend and boss, Dr. Miranda Sterling."

"A doctor, huh?"

"Yes, she is a Veterinarian, and a very good one if I say so myself!"

"That's interesting. So...how are you doing?"

"I'm doing well. Miranda and her little daughter, Taylor, have saved my life."

"What do you mean?" he asked sounding concerned.

"After you left me I went into a deep state of depression!"

"I'm sorry. I didn't mean to hurt you."

"Whether you meant to or not...you did!"

Changing the subject he asked, "Is this doctor friend of yours married?"

"No, her husband was killed a few years ago. She is now seeing to a wonderful man and I think they will eventually get married."

"That's nice. How about you? Are you dating anyone?"

Sallie had to laugh, "You're kidding, right?"

"No, I'm not kidding. You're still a beautiful and desirable woman."

"The man I love doesn't love me anymore," she said.

"I wouldn't go that far."

Sallie could tell he was getting a little nervous so she decided to end the conversation. "Take care of yourself and if you're ever in Medicine Bow drop in for a visit."

"Who knows? Maybe I will. Goodbye Sallie."

"I'm proud of the way you handled that Sallie," said Miranda.

"Thanks Miranda. I really didn't know what I would say to him if he called."

That was the end of the conversation and his name was not brought up again. Life went on as usual. The weekend was coming up and Miranda was excited.

After a nice weekend with Eli and Savannah at the ranch, Miranda was feeling more and more that he was the one for her. She didn't let him know though. She wanted to take it slow and be sure this time. He never hesitated to tell her he loved her. He was patient with her and never pushed for her to say the three words that he longed to hear from her lips. He knew she was the one for him and he would wait just as long as it took.

Monday morning Miranda went to work in a very cheerful mood. Little did she know that would not last very long. At ten o'clock she heard loud voices in the front office. She opened the door to see a strange woman talking loudly to Jade. "May I help you?" Miranda asked the woman in a pleasant voice.

"YOU'RE THE ONE I CAME TO SEE IF YOU'RE DR. STERLING!" she screamed.

"What can I do for you?"

"YOU CAN LEAVE MY MAN ALONE! THAT'S WHAT!"

"I don't understand," replied Miranda. "Who is your man?"

"It's Eli."

"Eli? I didn't know he was dating another woman!"

"He has been mine for a long time and I am not about to stand by and let another woman steal him from me!"

"I'm sorry...I still don't understand. Who are you?"

"My name is Serena."

"The same Serena that dumped Eli two weeks before the wedding?"

"Yes, it's me but I had a good reason for what I did."

"I'm sure you did," said Miranda. She'd about had enough of this woman. "For your information Eli and I are planning to get married!"

"YOU WHAT? I just came from his house and he never mentioned it."

"That's because he doesn't know yet. He will know before the day is over."

"YOU'LL MARRY HIM OVER MY DEAD BODY!!!" she screamed. "I DON'T WANT YOU TO EVER SEE

HIM AGAIN! IF YOU DO IT WILL BE THE LAST THING YOU EVER DO!!!"

"Are you threatening me?" asked a shaken Miranda.

"Call it what you want, but I am deadly serious!"

"You sound crazy to me!" exclaimed Miranda. "You need to leave before I call the police."

"I'm leaving but this is NOT over!" She turned and marched out the door.

"Whew," said Jade. "This was unexpected."

"Yes it was and uncalled for. I am going to call Eli right now and find out what's going on." She went back to her office and dialed his number. Lucky for her he answered. "Eli, it's Miranda. I just had a visitor!"

"You did?" he asked. "Who was it?"

"As if you don't know!" she said in an agitated voice. "I have just been threatened by your ex-fiancée!"

"WHAT?"

"That's right...she came over here. She threatened me and told me it was not over. She said she had been to your house."

"Yes, she was here and I told her there was no chance of us getting back together. I told her I had met someone new and was hoping you would marry me."

"Did you tell her my name?"

"No, I didn't have to. She already knew," he said.

"She lied to me. I told her we were planning to get married and she said you never told her."

"Yes, she did lie! Did I hear you say we are planning to get married? That's the very words I have been longing to hear!"

"I must confess...I am in love with you Eli, and I don't think there's any use in wasting more time."

"I totally agree with you! May I come over tonight? We need to start making plans."

"I would love for you to come over. Bring Savannah with you."

"I'll do just that. Meanwhile I am going to call the Sheriff's office and talk to them about Serena. If I have to I will get a restraining order against her."

"That would really set her off!"

"So be it. I will not have her threatening you or harming you in any way!"

"What if she shows up at our wedding?"

"Don't worry my love; I will take care of that. I plan to have a couple plain clothed deputies stationed nearby in the event of trouble."

"Good. That makes me feel better already."

Miranda felt better after talking with Eli. She felt so happy that he loved her and wanted to marry her. She was not going to let Serena put a damper on her happiness. In the meantime she would keep her eyes open because someone as crazy as Serena would not be above doing anything. She was not going to let that woman destroy what she had with Eli. She knew he was the man she had been waiting for and she was not going to hesitate about marrying him. God had given her a Second Chance at happiness and she was going to accept it.

She told Sallie her news before time for Eli to arrive. Sallie was so very excited and happy for her. "Will you be moving to the ranch?" asked Sallie.

"Yes."

"What about me?"

"I plan on keeping this apartment and if you'd like you can go on living here. I will bring Taylor to you each morning."

"I'm not sure I can afford it."

"Oh Sallie...I am not going to charge you rent. I am

paying for it. I just want you nearby. You are such a Godsend for Taylor and me!"

"Well I think this might work," she said smiling. "Thank you, Miranda! You are so generous!"

Eli and Savannah came over around seven o'clock that evening. While the girls played, Miranda and Eli planned their wedding. It was to take place out on the ranch. Miranda was so happy that he suggested it. Ranch living was her life! Karen would be her Matron of Honor. She would have Jennifer, Haley, Kati and Tammy, Eli's sister, as her Bridesmaids. Taylor and Savannah would be the Flower Girls. She knew she needed to go ahead and tell her family so they could make their travel plans. She called them later that night after Eli and Savannah were gone. Her sister and brothers were all excited and happy for her. She also talked to Gabe and asked him if he would give her away at which he said he would be happy to walk her down the aisle. After what had happened with Ethan they were all happy she had found true love once again. The girls were excited to be a part of Miranda's wedding. Miranda confirmed their dress and shoes sizes and told them she would be buying them.

The wedding was to take place in six months. That would give Miranda time to get everything lined up. The weather should be nice then and perfect for an outdoor wedding. She didn't want to wait later than July. The weather in Medicine Bow was unpredictable.

Eli's father, Bob, would be his Best Man. He and his wife Lori had four more sons, Tony, Travis, Tracy and Trent, who would be the Groomsmen. None of them lived in Medicine Bow. Work had taken them to other places. Eli was close to his parents and his siblings. He only had one sister, Tammy, who had grown up to be a tomboy since she had so many brothers. He was so happy they were all taking a part in his wedding.

She invited her friend Karen to go Wedding Gown shopping with her the next week. It would be a fun day out for the girls. They drove into Cheyenne to the Bridal Boutique where they browsed through many gowns. Miranda knew exactly what she was looking for. After searching and searching she was about to admit she needed to look somewhere else. Then...there is was! It was her dream dress. It was from the Jasmine Collection Style No. F203. It was an A-Line, Floor-Length, White/Ivory Satin, Empire Waist, Strapless Gown with Beading Embellishment and a Chapel Train. It was so Romantic yet Modern. Miranda knew this was her dress. Luckily they had it in Size 8 which fit her perfectly. She was so excited!

She also bought the needed wedding accessories, including her white satin shoes. She was glad to have that much taken care of. Now she could concentrate on the girls' dresses.

First they looked for Karen, Jennifer, Haley, Kati and Tammy a dress. Miranda was hoping she could find something in Emerald Green since that was her favorite color. This must be her lucky day. The sales lady showed her some new arrivals from her Wtoo Bridesmaid Collection and there it was...the perfect dress. It was the most gorgeous shade of emerald green. It was a Satin, Floor-Length dress with ruching around the waist which gave it a nice fitted look. There was also ruching on the off shoulder tiny sleeves. This was perfect! She was able to find all the sizes she needed. It's a good thing she was shopping early. She found strapless sandals in a lighter shade of green which would blend perfectly. Again luck was on her side. She found all the sizes she needed.

Next she looked at the Flower Girl dresses. Hoping to find something to blend in with the Bridesmaids' dresses, she kept searching. As she was looking in the Alfred Angelo section she spotted the cutest dress. It had an Emerald Green Satin tank with an Organza tea-length white skirt. A cascading organza flower sash accented the bodice color. This was perfect! Now for shoes...she found white sandals for both girls.

It was late that evening when the girls arrived back in Medicine Bow. It had been a fulfilling day for both girls. Before Miranda went to bed she called Eli to let him know she found the dresses and shoes. He was very happy. Then she called Jennifer, Haley, Kati and Tammy. They were excited too! She sure was thankful for Sallie who had already gotten Taylor into bed. She tiptoed into her baby's room and lightly gave her a kiss. She went back to her room and practically fell into bed. She was exhausted.

The next morning Sallie informed her that she'd had another call from Bobby. She had told him about Miranda's upcoming wedding in July. That was most of their conversation. Sallie had tried to avoid personal talk.

Chapter 19

Meanwhile Karen and Johnathan were planning their own wedding. They were getting married at the Medicine Bow Baptist Church. The wedding was to take place in May which was four months away. Karen had already bought a beautiful wedding gown. It was an A-line Satin dress featuring all-over lace embroidery. Its strapless Satin bodice was highlighted with a unique design which added a touch of romance and allure. She wanted to model it for Miranda. "WOW! What a beautiful bride you are going to be!" exclaimed Miranda.

"Thank you," replied Karen. "I am the luckiest girl in the world. I know Johnathan will make a wonderful husband. Patrick likes him too, which means a lot to me."

"I am so happy for you! Has my dress gotten here yet?" Karen had ordered their dresses off the internet.

"Yes, it came yesterday. That's why I called you over. I need for you to try it on and make sure it fits."

So Miranda proceeded to try on the Lavender Organza dress which fit perfectly. She didn't realize just how beautiful she looked. She was extremely happy for her best friend and didn't mind at all that Karen's wedding would occur before hers. She was to be the Maid of Honor. Two of Karen's other friends would be the Bridesmaids. Their dresses were in a deeper shade of purple with the styling similar to Miranda's.

Karen's son, Patrick, was giving her away. She was excited at that thought. It would be wonderful having her son walk her down the aisle.

Karen had asked Miranda if Taylor could be her Flower Girl. Miranda was happy to lend her little daughter to her best friend. The two of them took Taylor dress shopping in Cheyenne. They wanted to make sure they got the perfect fit. They found a lavender dress designed similar to Miranda's dress. They also found some lavender sandals.

Johnathan's nephew, Colton, would be the ring bearer. He was a year older than Taylor. They would be so cute together.

Everything was falling into place. Finally the BIG DAY came and everyone was dashing around making sure everything was in place. The church was decorated in shades of white baby's breath with lavender and purple flowers. It looked beautiful!

The wedding party took their place at the altar and waited for the beautiful Bride to walk down the aisle on her son's arm. Karen had a loving smile on her face as she kept her eyes focused on Johnathan. He had a winning smile on his face as he watched his gorgeous Bride make her way to him. He knew he was the luckiest man in the world!

It was a very special but short ceremony. The Bride and Groom were all smiles as they walked down the aisle and out the door. After congratulations to the couple, the guests all gathered in the Fellowship Hall for the reception.

Karen and Johnathan left the next day and went to Disney World for their honeymoon. Neither of them had been to Florida, so decided this would be a good opportunity to go.

Chapter 20

Karen and Johnathan had been married almost two months. She was busy helping Miranda with last minute details. It was only two weeks until the wedding. The last several months had been hectic for Miranda and Eli. There was so much to be done. Eli worked on the ranch getting things exactly like Miranda wanted them while she took care of the other aspects like hiring a band, photographer, and ordering the flowers. She had gotten in touch with Ethel and Emily at *Et & Em Catering* back home in Montana and they were excited about catering the wedding. It would give them a chance to visit their sister Sallie also. Things seemed to be going smoothly.

The day of the wedding was beautiful. The sun was shining brightly and the sky was a brilliant shade of blue. She could hear the birds singing their songs of melody in the surrounding trees. Miranda had to stop and take time to thank God for giving them such a wonderful day for their outdoor wedding. Had it been raining her plans would have changed. God was so good to her!

All of Miranda's family had gotten in two days ago. She was so happy to see them. Since there were so many of them, they were staying at THE VIRGINIAN HOTEL. They'd had a good time last night at the Wedding Rehearsal Dinner. Ethel and Emily had catered that also. They had arrived three days in advance and were staying at Miranda's house. Sallie was so happy to have them with her.

The guys unloaded the chairs and set them in place while the girls did what they needed to do. Everyone worked together so well and it all fell into place.

Finally it was time for the wedding. The crowd was gathering and the Groomsmen were escorting the ladies to their seats. After they were seated the wedding party came down the white carpet. Then all eyes were on the Bride as she slowly entered on the arm of her handsome brother-in-law, Gabe Colter. From the moment he saw her Eli never took his eyes off her. She was truly the most beautiful woman he had ever seen in his life. She took his breath away. As she approached and stood beside him, he turned to her and whispered I LOVE YOU. She smiled and whispered it back to him as their eyes locked. For one fleeting moment it was just the two of them and there was no one else around. Then reality set in and they turned their attention back to the minister.

They had written their own vows and as they professed their love for each other there was hardly a dry eye in the crowd. It was such a heart-warming ceremony. As the minister asked if anyone objected to the union of these two, a woman with long black hair and wearing dark glasses stood up. "YES I OBJECT! THESE TWO DO NOT BELONG TOGETHER. ELI IS MINE!!! HE IS GOING TO MARRY ME!!!"

At this point the two deputies realized this was the woman they were hired to be watching for. She sure had fooled them by wearing a black wig. They were looking for a blonde. They rushed over to her and slapped handcuffs on her and escorted her away from the ranch.

Meanwhile the minister seemed to be a little shaken but not as much as Miranda and Eli. He turned to Miranda and said, "I can't believe she had the nerve to do this."

"I can! She told me it wasn't over and I guess this is what she meant."

"Shall we proceed?" asked the minister.

Miranda and Eli both shook their heads YES. So he continued and at last pronounced them husband and wife. "Now you may kiss your Bride," he said looking at Eli.

Eli took his sweet time in doing this. As much as Miranda was enjoying it she could hear the crowd laughing and sort of pulled away from him. He smiled as he looked at her.

Miranda had a very special surprise when she looked around the crowd and saw her work partner, Dr. Laura Fisher, and husband, Shan, from Prince Edward Island. With them was their two year old son, Shan Jr. Miranda was so excited that she would finally get to see him. He had dark hair and very blue eyes. He was a carbon copy of his daddy. She was so happy they had been able to make it to her wedding.

On the last row sat an unknown man. He was dressed in a dark suit and was very handsome. He rose to his feet as the others did and got in line to congratulate the Bride and Groom. As he offered his congratulations Miranda said, "I don't think I know you. Are you new around here?"

He smiled and answered, "I just came for the wedding. My name is Bobby."

Miranda's mouth flew open, "BOBBY... as in Sallie's Bobby?"

He laughed and replied, "One and the same."

"I am really surprised to see you here. Does Sallie know?"

"I don't think so. I intend to find her though," he answered with a winning smile. He walked on and started searching the crowd. Finally he spotted her and made his way over to where she was standing with her sisters.

Sallie turned white when she saw him and began to feel dizzy. "I have to sit down," she said. Emily and Ethel saw him about the same time and weren't too happy that he showed up here.

"Hello, Ladies," he said with that smile he always wore.

"What are you doing here?" asked a stunned Sallie. "I thought I was seeing a ghost!"

"I came to see you," he laughed.

"Did you come alone?"

"Yes I did. I would like to talk to you."

"We can't talk here. Later you can come by where I live," she told him as she gave him the address. "Anyway, what is there left to talk about?"

"I just need to talk to you. I'll be by the house later," he said as he turned and walked away. He never stayed for the wedding reception. The reception he got from Sallie and her sisters told him that he actually wasn't welcome there. At this point he was wondering if he did the right thing by coming here. He got into his truck and drove back to Medicine Bow. He went to the diner on the corner and got a bite to eat.

Back on the ranch everyone was having a great time. The food was wonderful and plentiful. If anyone went away hungry it was their own fault. Ethel and Emily had outdone themselves with the food.

Miranda was in Heaven. She had just married her soul mate. Not only had she gained a wonderful husband but a great daughter as well. Savannah was such a sweet girl and would make a wonderful big sister for Taylor. For the little girl who didn't smile often, Savannah had come a long way. She kept a smile on her face now. She was so happy to have a new mommy and little sister.

Then Miranda's mind drifted back to the ceremony where Serena had interrupted. That was a nightmare! She wondered if the deputies had taken her to jail. If not she was still a threat. Miranda didn't trust her. She dreaded for Eli and herself to leave for their honeymoon. What if Serena tried to kidnap Taylor while she was gone…She had never forgotten the terror caused by the other kidnapping. She didn't ever want to go through that again. Then there was Savannah…She could possibly be in danger too. Sallie was going to come to the ranch and keep both of the girls.

"A penny for your thoughts," said a voice behind her as he wrapped his arms around her waist.

She turned to see her loving husband and reached up and gave him a kiss to which he replied, "You seem to be so far away my love."

"I guess I am Eli. I was thinking about Serena. Unless she is locked up she is still a threat to us! I am worried about leaving the girls with Sallie while we're gone. I guess I relive the nightmare of Taylor's kidnapping over and over."

"I'm so sorry Miranda!" he exclaimed. "I will call the Sheriff's Department and get an update."

"Thank you, Eli!"

He took out his cell phone and dialed the number. Miranda could tell by the way he was talking that it wasn't good. He got off the phone and gave her a sympathetic look. "I'm sorry Miranda but they didn't hold her. She got by with just a warning. If she bothers us again they will lock her up."

"Oh Dear Lord...what are we going to do?"

"The only thing left to do is hire a bodyguard. I'll contact the Sheriff and see if he can spare a deputy for the week we are gone."

"Oh that would make me feel so much better!" she exclaimed with a sigh.

"For now we need to get back to our wedding guests," said Eli.

"I know." They mingled and tried to speak a few words to everyone. This had been a wonderful day for both of them. Miranda was so glad that all her family could be here to share her special day. Her mind drifted back to another day her family shared her happiness at her wedding to Mardi Carson on Prince Edward Island. That seemed so long ago. She knew that Mardi would want her to move on and not spend the rest of her life grieving. She was so blessed that Eli came into her life when he did. She shuddered to think of how close she came to marrying Ethan. She would have lost Eli forever.

When all of the guests were gone Eli, Miranda and her family all gathered in the den of the beautiful 2 story log house on the ranch. They spent the rest of the evening catching up. They were all leaving on Monday morning so that meant they had one more day with their sister. Miranda was surprised that Blake Parker had time to fly in from Hollywood. He was still single and enjoying it. Even though he wasn't actually related to her, she still considered him as her brother. He was a half brother to Jennifer. He and Jordan were twins who had been separated at birth and reunited after they were grown.

Monday morning came and Miranda was sad to see her family leave. She now had a new family and was ready to start her life with them. Eli and Savannah would be a wonderful addition to their family. She was so thankful that God had directed her to move to Medicine Bow where she met Eli. If only Mardi could know...she knew he would be happy for her.

****

Meanwhile, back in Medicine Bow, Sallie, Emily and Ethel had gotten back to the apartment. They were having such a good time catching up when the doorbell interrupted them. Sallie got up and went to the door. There stood her ex-husband. "Come in," she said and closed the door behind him. "Have a seat."

He sat down looking very uncomfortable. The looks he was getting from Emily and Ethel were enough to make him uncomfortable. He wanted to talk to Sallie alone and how was he supposed to do that with her sisters hanging on to every word. Finally he spoke up, "Sallie, may I speak to you alone?"

Sallie looked at her sisters and asked," Would you mind?"

Emily and Ethel got up and went into the kitchen. Sallie was sure they would be quiet so they could hear what he had to say. That was okay because she would tell them when he left anyway.

Bobby got up from his seat and moved over to the sofa beside her. "I hardly know where to start but I have to tell you...I sure have missed you!"

Sallie looked at him with tears in her eyes and replied, "I've missed you too. I think of you every day."

"I know now that I did the wrong thing when I left you. I was such a fool!"

"What are you saying?"

"I'm saying that I would like to come back to you if you'll have me."

Sallie sat there too stunned to speak. This is what she had been hoping and praying for ever since he left her. She really didn't want a divorce but family members talked her into it. Now here he was asking to come home. What should she do? They weren't married anymore. He was married to another woman.

"I just don't know what to tell you, Bobby!" she exclaimed. "You hurt me so badly. You have no idea how much I grieved for you!"

"I'm so sorry that I hurt you!"

"How do I know you won't do it again?" she asked.

"I know you have no reason to trust me but I still love you. In fact, I don't think I ever stopped. I want to come back home."

"I'm not at home anymore. I live in Medicine Bow now."

"Can't you come back home to Montana?"

"Miranda needs me here to help with her young daughter Taylor. She has been so good to me and I can't turn my back on her when she needs me."

"Maybe I could come here."

"I think you need to end things with your wife before you even think of coming back to me!" exclaimed Sallie. "You can't have me and her too! I won't stand for that anymore!"

"I know..." he said with his head hung down."I feel so guilty for what I did to you. Can you ever forgive me?"

"I have already forgiven you. I can't be a Christian and not forgive you."

"You're a good woman, Sallie, and I was a fool to ever walk away from you! If you will take me back I promise I will NEVER hurt you again!"

"I can't give you an answer now. I will have to think about it and pray for God's guidance," she said as the tears ran down her face. She had hoped she wouldn't cry but she couldn't hold back the tears.

"That sounds fair enough. I will be waiting for an answer." With that he turned and walked out the door. She heard his truck start up and he drove away.

Little did he know that he took her heart with him. She walked into the kitchen with a saddened face. Emily and Ethel could tell she had been crying. Somehow she knew they had heard the conversation. "I just don't know what to do!" she exclaimed wiping a tear that trickled down her face.

"Don't rush into anything," said Emily. "Don't forget all the heartache he has caused you. Don't get involved with him while he is still married."

"I know...but in spite of everything I still love that man!"

"It's been a long and tiring day. I think I'll go to bed," said Emily.

"Me too," added Ethel. The two of them headed to the bedroom they were sharing.

Sallie sat in the living room for another hour just thinking and pondering the events of the day. Never in her wildest dream did she ever think Bobby would show up at Miranda's wedding. What am I going to do? She knew what her heart wanted to do but was it the logical thing to do? Could she stand the risk of being hurt again? She also knew if he was serious about coming back to her he would get a divorce first. She would wait and see... Meanwhile, she would pray and ask for God's guidance.

On Tuesday she left the apartment and drove to the ranch. She was staying with Taylor and Savannah while Miranda and Eli went on their honeymoon. She was so happy that things had worked out for them. She felt so relieved that Miranda hadn't married Ethan and waited for Eli. God had worked it all out. He never makes a mistake!

Miranda and Eli left the next morning and caught a plane to Maine. Neither of them had been there and thought this a good opportunity to go. Karen had talked so much about the state and that made Miranda more anxious to go see it.

They left the Casper/Natrona County International Airport early that morning. There was some delay at other airports but they finally reached their destination at the Portland International Airport. For the most part it had been a smooth flight. They were glad to get off the plane and stretch their legs. It was over 2,200 miles from Wyoming to Maine.

After a good night's rest they were up early and ready to do some touring. They had been looking forward to going on an Eagle Island Tour which they did on their first day. The 4-hour excursion included a 1 1/2 hour stopover on the Island. They learned that Eagle Island was the summer home of famed arctic explorer and Portland native Robert E. Peary, who claimed in 1909 to be the first person to reach the North Pole. There have been debates among arctic scholars, some of whom insisted he inflated his claims. According to sources, Peary built a simple home on a remote 17-acre island at the edge of Casco Bay in 1904. In 1912, he added flourishes in the form of two low stone towers. After his death in 1920, his family kept up the home; they later donated it to the state, which has since managed it as a state park. Since the home was open to the public they were able to see it. They were told it was maintained much like it was when Peary lived there.

Another interesting place they visited was the

Victoria Mansion. It was built between 1858 and 1860 for the wealthy Ruggles Morse and his wife Olivia. The Victoria Mansion, or Libby Morse as it is commonly known as, boasts a stunning architectural facade. It is the pride of Portland and houses some stunning remnants of pre-civil war era. It was a very beautiful mansion. They stopped by the gift shop and purchased some jewelry for Taylor, Savannah, Sallie and Karen. Eli bought Miranda a stunning necklace and earring set done in emerald green and silver. It caught his eye immediately. He knew it would match her green eyes but mostly because she looked so beautiful in that color.

They were having a wonderful time. The next stop was at Farnsworth Museum in Rockland. Despite its rough edges, Rockland has long and historic ties to the arts. Noted sculptor Louise Nevelson grew up in Rockland and in 1935 philanthropist Lucy Farnsworth bequeathed a fortune to establish the Farnsworth Museum, which has since become one of the most respected little art museums in New England. Located right downtown, the Farnsworth has a superb collection of paintings and sculptures by renowned American artists with connections to Maine - not only Nevelson, but also three generations of Wyeths (N.C., Andrew and Jamie), plus Rockwell Kent, Childe Hassam and Maurice Prendergast.

Another interesting point was the Pemaquid Point Lighthouse Park & Fishermen's Museum at Pemaquid. Featured on the state quarter, this historic lighthouse is visited by more than 100,000 people a year and possibly the most photographed lighthouse in Maine. It stands 35 feet tall and was erected in 1835. It became one of the first lighthouses with an automatic light in 1934. Miranda and Eli enjoyed touring the tower and visiting the Fishermen's

Museum where old photographs and artifacts tell the story of the town's maritime history.

In Wiscasset there was a fascinating museum at the edge of town overlooking the river. Castle Tucker was first built in 1807 in the style of a Scottish mansion, and then was radically added onto in 1858. The home remains more or less in the same state as it was in when reconfigured by cotton trader Captain Richard Tucker. Tours of the lower floors were offered by the Society of New England Antiquities, which was given the house by its former owner, Richard's daughter Jane in 1997. This was something to see. The extraordinary elliptical staircase was very beautiful and the painted plaster trim looked exactly like oak although it wasn't.

Miranda had searched the internet and found all this information on the places they were visiting. It was all so interesting. It was a great history lesson for them.

Miranda and Eli were having such a good time and home seemed so far away. They did call every night to check on their daughters. Everything seemed to be normal. They were so relieved that Serena had not caused any trouble.

Chapter 21

Back home in Medicine Bow things were about to change. Serena had been laying low and biding her time. She somehow knew Eli and Miranda's schedule. She waited until the night before their return, and then she headed for the ranch at dusk. Upon arriving she decided to park a good distance away and walk to the house. It was a hot night in July and she noticed the upstairs bedroom windows were open. She chuckled to herself and was thinking how luck was on her side. She ran her hand over her pocket to make sure the gun was still there. She meant business and she was going to make sure Eli and Miranda knew it.

She was very familiar with the layout of the house. She also knew what was in the barns and out buildings. She knew where to find the ladder she needed. Looking around and seeing no one, she went straight to that building and jiggled the door knob. As she expected it was locked. She withdrew a tool from her pocket and inserted it into the lock. In no time at all the door swung open. She smiled to herself. She proceeded to walk into the building, closed the door and sat down in a chair. She knew she had to wait until it was completely dark before carrying out her plans.

An hour or so later it was dark. She picked up the ladder and carefully carried it to the side of the house where the bedroom windows were open. She didn't realize the ladder was so heavy but she managed to get it there. Finally she had it propped up against the house. This is a piece of cake she was telling herself even though she was out of breath. She quietly climbed up the ladder and looked in the window. She couldn't see so she took her small flashlight from her pocket and shined it briefly on the bed. Wrong one she told herself. There was a woman in the bed. She turned off the light and climbed back down the ladder. She was puzzled. She was sure that was Savannah's room. She wasn't giving up... She moved the ladder to the next window and started to climb again. Taking out her flashlight again she shined it on the bed. BINGO! This was it! She could see not one but two little girls in the bed. She knew Savannah would be too big for her to handle so she opted for the smaller one. She quietly climbed through the window and tiptoed to the bed. She gently picked up Taylor and carried her toward the window. Taylor roused up for a few seconds, "Shhh..." said Serena in a whisper. "Everything is okay."

Taylor never said a word as Serena climbed out the window and descended the ladder holding onto the little girl until they reached the ground safely. In all this movement Taylor roused up again only to be comforted by Serena who reaffirmed her that all was well. As she was walking through the yard she tripped over a flower bush and fell, dropping Taylor onto the ground. Taylor immediately woke and began to cry loudly, "I WANT MY MOMMY!"

The deputy named Bill that Eli had hired was sleeping

on the sofa in the living room. He suddenly woke out of a deep sleep. He could hear Taylor crying for her mommy. He jumped to his feet, grabbed his gun and headed out the front door. "Who's there?" he yelled. "Come out with your hands up!"

About that time a shot pierced the air. The deputy let out a yell and fell to the ground. He had been hit in the leg. He could hear movement as if someone was running away. He was unable to stand up. By now Sallie had heard the commotion and was running out the front door. "WHAT'S GOING ON?"

"I've been shot. We've had a burglar and I think it's also a kidnapping!"

"OH NO...NOT TAYLOR!!! NOT AGAIN!!!" screamed Sallie.

"Go call 911. We need to get the police on this as soon as possible."

Sallie ran back into the house and grabbed the phone. She quickly dialed the number and waited for the sheriff to answer. She was so frantic she could hardly talk. Finally, she got the message relayed to him and he said he would get right on it.

She ran back outside and asked the deputy what she could do for him. He had already taken off his belt and made a tourniquet to slow down the bleeding.

"Call the doctor and ask him to meet me at his office. Will you drive me there?"

"Of course. I'll go wake up Savannah."

Twenty minutes later they pulled into the Medicine Bow Medical Clinic parking lot. Dr. Stansbery was already there. Sallie helped Bill into the waiting room and the doctor immediately took him into his office. Thirty minutes later the bullet was out and his leg was bandaged.

Bill walked out on crutches. Dr. Stansbery helped him into the car and Sallie drove him home.

It was getting late but Sallie knew she had to make that dreaded call to Miranda and Eli. Sallie hardly knew how to break the news to them. She knew Miranda would go to pieces. Why did this have to happen to her again? She is such a wonderful person... then it dawned on her that 'Bad Things Happen to Good People' too.

Sallie was relieved when Eli answered Miranda's phone. He saw it was the home number and was quite startled that they would be calling this late at night. Before she could say anything he anxiously asked, "What's the matter Sallie?"

"It's bad, Eli!" she exclaimed. "Someone climbed up a ladder into the girl's room and took Taylor!"

"WHAT???" DID YOU CATCH THEM?"

"I'm afraid not. The burglar shot Bill in the leg and we just got back from Dr. Stansbery's office."

"Did you call 911?" he asked.

"Yes, I called before taking Bill to the doctor. Sheriff Ethan said he would get right on it."

"Good! You did the right thing! Miranda and I will be leaving in the morning. Please watch Savannah closely until we get there. Thanks and goodnight, Sallie."

Eli dreaded telling Miranda about the phone call but knew he couldn't avoid it.

"Who was that on the phone?" she asked.

"It was Sallie." He told her everything Sallie had told him and tears came to her eyes as she whispered, "Dear God...NOT again!"

Eli went to her and held her in his arms and tried to comfort her. "Did they see who it was?"

"No, it was too dark."

"Well I KNOW!!! It was Serena! She told me this

wasn't over and I knew that sooner or later she would strike again. This time she is in serious trouble... especially if I find her!"

"The police are looking for her. I'm sure Ethan has put out an APB on her. They'll catch her."

"She's as dangerous as a Rattlesnake, Eli! I don't trust her for one minute and to think she has my baby girl!" She couldn't hold the tears any longer. She cried until there were no tears left. Eli held her and tried to comfort her.

"We need to pray for Taylor's safety and I believe that God will bring her back home to us."

Miranda never slept any even though she lay in bed beside Eli the rest of the night. She was up at five o'clock getting ready for their early flight back to Medicine Bow. Both of them were praying for Taylor.

They boarded the plane and arrived in Casper in the late afternoon. After collecting their luggage they headed for their car that they had left on the airport parking lot. It was a long ride home. When they arrived, Sallie was the first one out the door to greet them. She had a big smile on her face. They wondered what was making her so happy. Then they saw what it was. Not far behind them came a blonde haired little girl of three years old followed by Savannah.

Miranda ran as fast as she could screaming, "TAYLOR!!!" She grabbed her baby girl up into her arms and hugged and kissed her like there was no tomorrow. "When did they find her? Tell me everything!"

So Sallie explained it all to them. "Serena had been spotted in a diner just a few hours ago. Police surrounded the diner and they arrested her. They took little Taylor from her and one policeman brought her back to us on the ranch. A couple of other deputies took Serena to jail. They say she will not get off this time. Breaking and entering, shooting an officer, and kidnapping are serious offenses. Frankly I hope they lock her up and throw away the key," she said laughing.

"I agree with you 100%, Sallie!" exclaimed Miranda.

"I just can't understand what happened to her," said Eli. "To think I almost married her...well that gives me the chills."

"Just be thankful she broke off the engagement when she did. I know you suffered but your suffering would have been much worse if you had married her."

"I agree with you Miranda. I know God was certainly looking out for me. He knew she was the wrong woman for me. Besides...He was keeping me for YOU!"

"I'm so glad He did," she answered as she gave him a kiss. Her world was complete now. She had a wonderful husband and two beautiful daughters. God had been so good to them.

Chapter 22

The next several months went by and Sallie never heard a word from Bobby. She was deeply hurt and told herself it was better this way.

One morning a little over six months after Miranda's wedding, there was a knock on the door. Miranda had already brought Taylor to her for that day. She wondered who it could be. She went to the door only to find Bobby standing there with a big grin gracing his face. Sallie grabbed her chest as her mouth was gaping open. "BOBBY!!!" she exclaimed in a surprised tone of voice and big eyes. "What are you doing here?"

"I've come back to you if you want me!" he exclaimed.

Tears welled up in her eyes as she asked him to come in. "This is such a shock. I didn't think I would ever hear from you again."

"I had a lot to do before I could come back. I left my wife and we are now divorced," he said as he pulled the divorce papers out of his coat pocket and handed them to Sallie.

With a stunned look on her face she accepted the

papers and unfolded them. As she read them tears of joy filled her soul. She could not believe this was happening. She handed the papers back to him and sat down on the sofa. Her legs were about to collapse under her. So much was happening and it was almost more than she could take. She felt like she was in another world. She closed her eyes for a moment and thanked God for answering her prayer.

Bobby sat down beside her and placed his arm around her shoulder. "Don't be sad," he said. "I am back where I belong. I won't ever leave you again and that's a promise."

She turned and looked him straight in the eye and replied, "I want to believe you so badly. I still can't believe it's true."

"Maybe time will change all that!" he exclaimed. He leaned over and gave her a brief kiss. She smiled so sweetly at him. He then pulled her close to him and kissed her again. This time it was not a brief kiss. It took her back to what they had long ago. The love she had felt for him for all those years came creeping back instantly. She knew she would always love this man no matter what. When they married years ago she had given him her heart and body. There was never anyone else for her. She was still in shock that he had come back to her. She never dreamed that would ever happen.

"Sallie, will you marry me again?" he asked earnestly.

"Yes I will, Bobby. In my heart we are still married. I know in the eyes of the law we were divorced but in my heart we always belonged to each other."

"Let's get married as soon as possible!" he exclaimed. "I don't see any need in putting it off!"

"I agree with you. Do you have to go back home and get your belongings?"

"No, I brought my clothes and a few other things. That's all I need. We will make a fresh start here in Medicine Bow."

"I like the sound of that," she said smiling.

"Do you know a minister who can marry us?"

"My friend Karen got married at Medicine Bow Baptist Church. I'm sure we could get that minister. I will give Karen a call."

"Sounds good."

He stayed there with her and Taylor all day. He was fascinated with Taylor who made up with him right from the beginning. When Miranda came to pick up Taylor after work she was surprised that Sallie had company. After explaining everything to Miranda she asked if she wanted her to move out of the apartment after she and Bobby got married.

"Of course not!" exclaimed Miranda. "That won't change a thing. You'll just have someone to help you." She looked at Bobby and winked. "It will be good for you to have someone with you."

"I know," replied Sallie. "I still can't believe this has happened and the best part is he has asked me to marry him again!"

"I think that's great!" exclaimed Miranda. "Do you have a date set?"

"As soon as possible," replied Bobby. "There's no use in waiting!"

"I am going to ask Karen to contact her minister and see if he will marry us right away," said Sallie. "We don't want a big wedding."

"Let me set up everything up for you Sallie," suggested Miranda.

"That would be wonderful, Miranda," replied Bobby. "Sallie and I appreciate that very much!"

Miranda contacted the minister of the Medicine Bow Baptist Church who said he would be happy to perform the wedding ceremony. The wedding was planned for the first week in March. Since winters were so cold and snowy Emily and Ethel decided not to come. They sent their congratulations to their sister and told her they would see her when the weather got warm again.

So on the first Saturday of March, Bobby and Sallie once again joined hands in matrimony. This time it felt different. They both realized this was their last chance at happiness. They weren't young anymore and life was swiftly passing. They had no children and as they looked back they realized they would grow old alone... but together.

Miranda, Eli, Savannah, and Taylor were there for them, as well as Karen and Johnathan. These were very special people to Sallie. She loved them all dearly. The one she loved most of all had come back to her. She just couldn't thank God enough for sending him back home to her. No matter how many years she had left she knew she would no longer be alone. She thanked God for second chances.

Chapter 23

Shortly after Sallie and Bobby's wedding, Miranda woke up one morning feeling like she had the flu. She was too sick to stay up. As soon as her feet hit the floor she was nauseated. She called Sallie and asked her if she could come to the ranch and keep Taylor. Sallie quickly agreed and arrived less than an hour later. This went on the rest of the week. Miranda was beginning to wonder why the flu was lasting so long when usually it was over in twenty-four hours. After five days of feeling so nauseated, Miranda wondered if it could be something else. Then it hit her like a ton of bricks! I'M PREGNANT!

She knew that Eli would like to have another child so they hadn't prevented it. Why didn't she realize it before now? She thought it probably wouldn't happen this soon since it took her so long to get pregnant with Taylor. It had happened and she was thankful. She knew it was in God's plans. She decided to drive into Medicine Bow to the pharmacy and buy an EPT. She wanted to be sure before telling Eli.

The next morning she got up and got ready for town. She took Taylor and off they went. She was thinking about it as she drove the ten miles into Medicine Bow. She thought about stopping in to see Karen but decided it wouldn't be fair to Eli to tell her first. She didn't want to hurt him. So they hurried back home and after she got Taylor settled in her playroom she headed for the bathroom. She sat in anticipation waiting for the results of the pregnancy test. She was almost afraid to look. As she turned her head and rested her eyes upon the results she let out a yell.

Taylor came running into the bathroom. "What's wrong, Mommy?"

"Oh nothing, Taylor. Mommy is just happy! You can go back and play now."

"Okay, Mommy." She left the room in a run and went back to play.

She could hardly wait for Eli to come for lunch today. She sure was glad he was working near the house. Sometimes when he was repairing fences he would have her pack his lunch so he could save time. She was always at her clinic anyway. She had closed it for a week or so during her illness.

Finally it was noon and she heard him coming in the back door. She went downstairs to meet him. "What are you doing out of bed?" he asked. "Are you feeling better?"

"Yes, I am feeling much better. I think you will also when you hear what I have to say."

He gave her a strange look and asked, "What is it?"

"What would you say if I told you that you are going to be a daddy again?"

"WHAT???" He came over and took her in his arms. "Are you sure?"

"I think so. I just took an EPT and it was positive."

"That's the BEST news ever! You need to go to the

doctor and let him confirm it so you can start pre-natal care."

"I know and I will in a few days."

"Miranda, you have made me so happy! I am very proud of our daughters and couldn't love Taylor any more if she were mine. God has been so good to us! Now He is blessing us with another baby...together. Wouldn't it be nice if we could have a boy this time?"

"That's what I've been thinking, but we will accept what the Lord gives us. He knows exactly what we need."

Miranda went back to work the following Monday but took time to go see Dr. Stansbery. She had thought about seeing an OB/GYN but she would have to drive a great distance. Most of the women in Medicine Bow used the local doctor.

Dr. Stansbery told her that everything looked great and she was two months pregnant. He saw no reason why she couldn't continue her work at the vet clinic. He told her not to lift heavy animals but have her assistant to help. That was no problem.

Miranda had waited until after going to the doctor before telling her family the great news. They were all so excited for her and Eli. It would be nice to have another addition to the family. She promised to keep them informed every step of the way.

A couple more months passed and it was time for an Ultrasound. Eli went with her to the doctor that day. He was as excited as she was. It never took the doctor long to find out the sex of the baby. "Mr. & Mrs. Warren...you are having a baby boy!"

"YES!!!" exclaimed Eli loudly. He was beaming like a new daddy.

"I am so happy too!" exclaimed Miranda. She turned her head and fastened her eyes on Eli. "I am so thankful that I can give you the much desired son you have been longing for!"

"I want Elijah to be part of his name," said Miranda smiling at her handsome husband.

"What about THOMAS ELIJAH WARREN? Thomas was my grandfather's name."

"I love it! You have just named our son!"

"We can call him Tommy while he is small and I'm sure he will shorten it to Tom as he gets older."

"That's fine with me."

They could hardly wait to tell Savannah and Taylor that they were going to have a baby brother. Savannah was at school and Taylor was at Sallie's house. Miranda knew she had to stop in and tell Sallie immediately. As the two of them walked in the front door Sallie could tell something was going on. "Good News?" she asked.

"YES, we have great news!!!" exclaimed Miranda. "Eli and I are going to have a baby boy!"

"Oh that is great! I am so happy for you!"

Miranda told Taylor who didn't seem to care one way or another. Being that young, a baby is a baby. Savannah would understand better.

They left Sallie's house and went to see Karen. She was busy working but took time to hear the good news. "I am so happy for you both! He will be lucky to have two big sisters to help take care of him."

"Indeed he will," said Miranda.

As soon as they got home, Miranda called her family. She talked to Jennifer first, as usual. They were very close even though they were only half sisters. Jennifer was very excited when she heard that Miranda was carrying a baby boy. She loved the name they had picked out also.

Miranda called her other siblings then decided to call Dr. Laura Fisher. They had a nice conversation and

Laura wished them the best. "Little boys are lots of fun," she added with a laugh. "You never know what they are carrying in their pants pocket. It might be a frog, a bug, a worm or God forbid...a baby snake. I really have to watch Shan Jr. Little boys are unpredictable."

"I'll try to be prepared," Miranda laughed.

The next seven months went by quickly. Everything seemed to be going well with Miranda's pregnancy except she felt tired most of the time. She decided to cut her work hours and only work three days a week...Monday, Wednesday and Friday. That way she would have a day to rest between her work days. That worked out well for her. In case of an emergency she would open the clinic and accommodate her patients. That only happened twice during those seven months.

Her due date was approaching quickly. She was hoping all would go well since she was having her baby in the birthing section of Dr. Stansbery's clinic. Had she planned to drive to Casper to the hospital she might not have made it in time. This seemed to be the best thing for her and she trusted Dr. Stansbery completely. His wife, Shirley, was a Registered Nurse and would be assisting him in the delivery. She knew she would be in good hands.

Two days before her due date she went into labor at seven o'clock that night. She immediately called Sallie who said she would be right over. Bobby was bringing her and would stay with them. They arrived about twenty minutes later and Eli and Miranda were ready to leave. It was before eight o'clock when they pulled into the clinic parking lot. Eli jumped out and ran around to open her door and help her out. Once they got inside, Dr. Stansbery and Shirley took over. Eli dropped into a seat in the waiting room.

"We'll call you when we have her ready," said Shirley with a loving smile.

"Thanks," replied Eli with a worried look on his face.

It wasn't long until Eli was invited into the delivery room. He was perspiring something terrible. They could tell he was really nervous. After talking to him they realized this was his first delivery that he had been a part of. "She's going to be fine," said Shirley trying to calm him down. "Try not to worry. Just think...you're about to be a new father!"

"I know and I am very excited!"

Everything was going well with Miranda and she was pushing and breathing as she remembered doing with Taylor. She took one look at Eli and realized she was in better shape than he was. Deep inside...she giggled! She was thinking to herself and knew this was exactly why woman are the ones who give birth. Then a very sharp pain hit her and she moaned as she grabbed Eli's hand so tightly that it almost cut off his circulation. He thought he was going to faint. His head was getting dizzy and he grabbed the side of the bed with his other hand to keep from falling. "Help me Lord," he mumbled under his breath.

"PUSH!" exclaimed Dr. Stansbery. "GOOD GIRL! A couple more like that and the baby will be out."

Miranda was cooperating and in a few minutes it was over. She felt her body go limp. She could now relax...her work was over. She had once again delivered a precious baby but this time it was a son. The doctor laid the baby on her stomach for them to see. He was perfect! Eli was beside himself with excitement. He now had a son...the son he had longed for!

Nurse Shirley cleaned the baby and weighed him. He weighed 8 lbs. 2 oz. He was off to a good start. He was breathing on his own and everything seemed to be normal about him. Eli was still holding Miranda's hand as he bowed his head in prayer. He thanked God for his wonderful wife and for the beautiful baby son she had just borne. He also thanked God for allowing him to stand on two feet and not hit the floor. He promised God that they would raise their son according to His will. He asked for protection and blessings on their family of five. When he finished he bowed down and kissed Miranda then said, "I love you, Miranda! Thank you for loving me and for giving me a beautiful son. God has been so good to me. I never dreamed I would ever be this happy. I am so glad you came to Medicine Bow!"

"Me too!" she exclaimed. "I know God had His hand in my life and guided me here. He knew you were here waiting for me." She gave him a smile that almost melted his heart.

"THANK YOU, JESUS!!!" he exclaimed.

"Mr. Warren," said Shirley. "You might as well go home and get some rest tonight. You can come back tomorrow afternoon to pick up your wife and son if all is well."

"Thanks, Shirley." He said goodnight to Miranda and little baby Tommy and left.

Early the next afternoon Eli came strolling through the door with a big grin on his face. He sure was one proud daddy! Shirley helped Miranda get her things together while Eli pulled the car up close to the front door. They got everything loaded and headed for the ranch.

Sallie and Taylor were waiting for them. Savannah was still at school. Taylor was so excited to see her mommy and looked surprised when she saw her daddy with the baby carrier. She had been told they were getting a new baby but reality had not set in until now. Seeing him in person was much different than hearing about a baby. The countenance on her face changed as she caught the first glimpse of her baby brother. "He's little!" she exclaimed.

Looking up at her mommy she asked, "Can we keep him?"

"Sure we can keep him. He's your little brother and his name is Tommy. You and Savannah are going to make wonderful big sisters for him."

"I like Tommy," she said as she touched his tiny face.

"Of course you do and Tommy will love you too when he gets old enough to know you. For now you need to help Mommy and Daddy take good care of him."

"OKAY... I CAN DO THAT!" she exclaimed ever so proudly.

Savannah was equally excited when she got home from school. The first thing she wanted to do was hold her baby brother. Eli sent her to wash her hands, and then she could hold the baby. When Miranda placed little Tommy in her arms she grinned from ear to ear. She had never been around a baby so this was all new to her. She touched his fingers and he grabbed her finger. "Look!" she shouted. "He's holding my finger!"

"Babies love to do that," said Miranda. "I think it makes them feel secure."

With a look of total confidence Savannah spoke up, "Tommy will never have to feel insecure. I will make sure of that."

"You'll be a good big sister and I am so proud of you!" exclaimed her beaming dad.

"God has surely blessed us with our wonderful children!" exclaimed Miranda.

"Indeed He has," added Eli. "I feel so humble in His sight and can never thank Him enough for all the blessings He has given me. Before I met you and Taylor, it was just Savannah and me. Now we are a family of five!"

"Yes, God has truly blessed us. I never dreamed I would have a second chance at love, especially with a wonderful husband like you, Eli. Then God gave us this beautiful love child. I can finally put my past to rest and dream about my future with you and our three children. I have no doubt in my mind that I made the right choice when I came to MEDICINE BOW. It is truly a NEW BEGINNING for me."

About the Author

Sally Campbell Repass is a devoted wife, mother, grandmother and great-grandmother. She has been married to her loving husband, Paul, for 10 years. They are going through a very difficult time now, as he battles Stage IV Colon cancer. Their faith in God, the love of family and dear friends, has helped ease the pain.

Sally wrote and published a Children's Fairytale Book, '*Princess Kari* & *The Golden Haired Boy*' in early 2010. This book was inspired by her granddaughters, Katie and Campbell.

Later that year, she published her first Inspirational Romance Book, '*For The Love Of Rachel*'.

In 2011 she followed with a sequel, '*Rachel's Daughter*'.

Not being able to let go of the family she had created, she decided to write a third book.

In 2012, '*From The Ranch...To The Island*' was born.

Her fourth book in the series was also published in 2012.

'*Back Home To Montana*' is the continuing saga of the Parker/Sterling families.

Now Book #5 in the series has been published. '*Medicine Bow...A New Beginning*' brings about a turn of events.

Book #6 will be the final one in this series. As the book ends, so will the saga of this family she has grown to love. She has spanned 4 generations of the Parker/Sterling families and hopes you have enjoyed the journey as much as she has.

Website: www.fortheloveofrachel.com

Email: virginiawriter2010@gmail.com
screpass2008@yahoo.com